AN EXTRAVAGANT MERCY

An Extravagant Mercy

Reflections on Ordinary Things

M. Craig Barnes

SERVANT PUBLICATIONS
ANN ARBOR, MICHIGAN

Vine Books is an imprint of Servant Publications especially designed to serve evangelical Christians.

Servant Publications—Mission Statement

We are dedicated to publishing books that spread the gospel of Jesus Christ, help Christians to live in accordance with that gospel, promote renewal in the church, and bear witness to Christian unity.

Published in association with the literary agency of Alive Communications, Inc., 7680 Goddard Street, Suite 200, Colorado Springs, CO 80920.

Published by Servant Publications
P.O. Box 8617
Ann Arbor, Michigan 48107
www.servantpub.com

Cover design: Noah Pudgil Design Professionals

03 04 05 06 10 9 8 7 6 5 4 3 2 1

Printed in the United States of America
ISBN 1-56955-370-X

Library of Congress Cataloging-in-Publication Data

Barnes, M. Craig.
   An extravagant mercy : reflections on ordinary things / M. Craig Barnes.
      p. cm.
   ISBN 1-56955-370-X (alk. paper)
   1. Bible--Theology--Meditations. I. Title.
   BS543.B355 2003
   242'.5--dc21

2003004716

Contents

Preface

For over nine years I had the great honor of serving as the pastor of The National Presbyterian Church in Washington, D.C. One of the hallmarks of my ministry there was to invite my congregation into the life-transforming practice of beginning each day alone with God in prayer and Bible reading.

To assist the members of the congregation in this practice, I encouraged them to follow the biblical readings as assigned by the Common Daily Lectionary. On the back page of our Sunday worship bulletin, one column listed the lectionary readings for each day of the upcoming week. Next to that column was a long red box that contained a devotional I had written, based on one of the biblical readings from the previous week. *An Extravagant Mercy* is a compilation of these weekly devotionals.

I never thought that these devotional writings would have a life beyond the Sunday morning in which they appeared in the worship bulletin. And to tell the truth, I wrote them for the sheer joy of it as much as because I thought it would help inculcate the practice of daily worship in the congregation. But the gracious elders of National Presbyterian chose to bind together a couple of slim volumes of the devotionals, each titled *Grace and Peace,* for distribution through the congregation. When the equally gracious editors of Servant Publications were given these two volumes, they cleaned up the writing, gleaned the best selections, regrouped them, and have now published them together in this single edition.

Since writing these devotionals, I have resigned my position as a parish pastor in order to teach the art of pastoral ministry at Pittsburgh Theological Seminary. While I am greatly enjoying serving as a professor, I miss some of my old routines of pastoral ministry—none more than the Sunday night practice of writing the devotional that would appear in the next week's bulletin. As I now review these writings I am struck by a few things.

First, it is a good discipline for writers to contain their thoughts to a little red box on a page. That box in the worship bulletin permitted only about 285 words. As a result, these devotionals don't waste words. The reader may even wish I had included a few more. But to that I would say, "Think of this writing as only the beginning of your own conversation with God."

Second, the reader will benefit by reading this book slowly. The selections have been carefully arranged by the publisher to provide continuity of theme, but to plow through too many of the selections at one sitting will only diminish the contribution of any one of them. *An Extravagant Mercy* is not so much a book to be read as a collection of devotional thoughts on specific portions of the Bible. And since these little devotionals were written to accompany the reading of Holy Scripture, they don't hold up well apart from the biblical texts, nor are they sufficient to guide anyone into deeper spirituality if they are used as a substitute for prayer and Bible reading.

The third and most important thing this volume of devotionals illustrates is that my ministry as a pastor has been dominated by awe over the extravagant mercy of God. I find it everywhere, as does any pastor who is paying attention to the lives of parishioners. My prayer is that as you slowly make your way through these devotionals, you too will learn to attend to the many ways God is transforming the ordinary things of life into the means of his extravagant grace.

ONE

Grace: God Beyond the Boundaries

❦

Shaken to Our Foundations

Are we to continue in sin that grace may abound? By no means!
Romans 6:1-2, RSV

READ ROMANS 6:1-23

The whole concept of grace is confusing to us. That is particularly unfortunate since it is pretty much the fundamental point of the gospel. We can at least take comfort in knowing that the Romans had a hard time understanding it as well. The apostle Paul spent most of his letter to the Romans explaining God's grace over and over again. It is as if to say that an illustration of how badly we need grace is the fact that we can't quite understand it.

Grace is better than the fulfillment of all our dreams. It is the fulfillment of God's dream—our forgiveness. Grace means that God gives us what we need and not what we deserve.

It isn't really a difficult concept to understand, but that is not what confuses us. It's the gift that we can't quite accept. Do we really want what we don't deserve? We may not have been perfect, but we certainly have been careful. Don't we deserve something for trying so hard?

Trust me on this. When it comes to standing before God, getting what we deserve is the last thing we want.

Receiving God's grace shakes the very foundations of our carefully constructed lives. It calls us to start all over and begin to live a passionate drama with this lover God who will do anything to save us. We even have to lose our interest in carefully constructed lives because, well, that may be the greatest sin of all.

9

❦

Sometimes a Raging River

They are like trees planted by streams of water.

Psalm 1:3

READ PSALM 1

The Bible often portrays the grace of God as a thin stream of refreshing water that perseveres in a desert land. The only way our parched souls can survive in a spiritually desolate society is to stay close to that stream. That is why we come to worship, read our Bibles, serve others, and pray without ceasing throughout the day. It's all a way of drinking in the grace that keeps us spiritually alive. The more time we spend by that stream, the more deeply our lives become rooted in God.

Those roots are pretty important because sometimes we get more grace than we want. It doesn't happen often, but when the storms come, the thin stream can suddenly turn into a raging river, washing away everything that is not firmly planted. We never want to get too sentimental about grace. While most days it is God's gentle refreshment to our souls, some days it comes as a terrifying reminder that our lives are out of control.

On the stormy days, we may wonder if it was such a good idea to live so close to the stream. We may even wish God would just leave us alone. Yet if the torrent sweeps away the things that are not spiritually rooted, then even that is a grace. Remember, the point of God's grace is not to be nice to us. Grace does what we cannot do for ourselves. It carries us home to God. Sometimes on a gentle stream. Sometimes on a raging river. Yet always back to God.

❦

In Too Deep

I have swept away your transgressions like a cloud, and your sins like mist; return to me, for I have redeemed you.

Isaiah 44:22

READ ISAIAH 44:21-23

Notice that the Lord doesn't say, "Return to me and I will redeem you." No, this verse makes it clear that we are able to return home to God only because he has already redeemed us. Our sins have been swept away. They're gone, without a trace. That is why Jesus' last words on the cross included the phrase, "It is finished." There is nothing we can do to add to our salvation.

I think that the reason Jesus enjoyed hanging around really big sinners was because they knew it was impossible to return to God by trying to clean up their lives a bit. They were in too deep. Grace was their only hope. By contrast, those who were making some progress on the road of spirituality by trying harder never quite understood Jesus. And they never quite made it home. None of us is going to get there without forgiveness.

In Christ, we have already received all the grace necessary for the journey home to the heavenly Father. So it is pointless to drag a lot of guilt behind us on the way home. It slows us down and makes it impossible to enjoy the journey. It also makes it impossible for others to enjoy being on the journey with us. Anyway, once we arrive we're just going to have to leave the guilt at the door, because the heavenly Father doesn't allow it in his house.

✦

God Beyond the Boundary

When he came and saw the grace of God, he rejoiced.

Acts 11:23

READ ACTS 11:1-26

The first missionary strategy of the church of Jerusalem was to preach the gospel to the Jews who were living in Jerusalem. Yet the church was severely persecuted in Jerusalem, so many followers of Jesus fled to places like Antioch. The second missionary strategy was then to preach to the Jews who were living in these places as well. However, some people began to preach to Gentiles in Antioch without authorization, and a great number of these Gentiles became believers and turned to the Lord. That was not in the plan.

When the church in Jerusalem heard about all these Gentile converts, it sent Barnabas to Antioch to straighten out this problem. Yet when Barnabas saw that it was the grace of God that was converting these Gentiles, he rejoiced and welcomed them into the faith. Then he found Paul in Tarsus, and together they became the first dynamic missionary team to the Gentiles. So Barnabas, who was supposed to fix the problem of Gentile converts, ended up becoming part of the problem. However, the real problem for the church leaders in Jerusalem was that the grace of God was operating outside of their strategic plan.

To be of use to God, we will need to make careful plans for what we want to accomplish. Remember, however, that plans create boundaries, and often God is at work outside of those boundaries. So we will have to make changes. It will be a lot easier to change our plans than to change the plans of God.

✤

Thrown to the Dogs

"It is not fair to take the children's food and throw it to the dogs."

Mark 7:27

READ MARK 7:24-30

After feeding the five thousand, healing the sick, teaching the crowds, and arguing with the Pharisees, Jesus was tired. He was ready for a little retreat. Mark tells us, "He entered a house and did not want anyone to know he was there." However, a Gentile woman found out where he was hiding. She threw herself at Jesus' feet and begged him to cast a demon out of her daughter. Reminding her that she was not Jewish, Jesus said that would be like taking the children's bread and throwing it to the dogs.

This is a harsh statement. Some have suggested it was Jesus' fatigue that was speaking here. When we're really tired we tend to be less gracious and more irritable. Sometimes we become focused on our mission and limitations. "I just do Jews. No Gentiles." Yet, let me suggest another interpretation. Jesus said what he said because he meant it. The woman really didn't deserve Jesus' healing. Neither do you or I.

Notice that the Gentile woman didn't argue with Jesus. That's because she knew he was right. It wouldn't be fair for Jesus to give her a thing. Yet when we're in need of grace, the last thing we want is what is fair. Instead, the woman reminded Jesus that even the dogs got scraps that fell from the table. Jesus was so impressed that he healed her daughter on the spot. That's because Jesus never tires of saving those who understand the power of even a little grace.

❦

The Familiar Stranger

Then their eyes were opened, and they recognized him; and he vanished from their sight.

Luke 24:31

Read Luke 24:13-35

After the crucifixion, Cleopas and another discouraged follower of Jesus were walking down the road on the way to Emmaus. Along the way they were joined by the risen Jesus, but neither of them recognized him. The resurrection appearances of Jesus were all so unspectacular. Mary thought he was just the cemetery gardener. Peter thought he was just a man interested in his catch of fish. Cleopas thought he was just a stranger along the road.

Grace, the hopeful intervention of God in our lives, always shows up as a stranger. Often the stranger is unwelcome. Maybe it is failure, something unfamiliar to us. Yet this strange thing appears to proclaim that life is too short to collect trophies, and in the failure we at last find the freedom to enjoy life. Maybe the stranger is a painful grief, but as we walk through it, we discover a Savior walking beside us. I don't know what the stranger may look like to you, but if it is the risen Christ who is coming, clearly he won't look the way you expected. After the disciples' eyes were opened to see that the stranger was Jesus, he then vanished from sight. It was no longer necessary to see him to know he was with them. He was no longer the unrecognized visible presence. Now he was the recognized invisible presence.

None of us knows what is waiting down the road. We can handle that as long as we know Jesus is also waiting, even if we can't always see him.

❧

Perfect Power

So I will boast all the more gladly of my weaknesses, so that
the power of Christ may dwell in me.

2 Corinthians 12:9

READ 2 CORINTHIANS 12:1-10

The apostle Paul once gave thanks to God for a thorn that was stuck
in his flesh. He had begged God to pull it out. He had prayed about
it repeatedly. Still, the thorn remained. We don't know what it was. It
may have been a physical limitation or a painful memory. It may have
been another person who drove him crazy.

I think it is good that Scripture doesn't fill in this blank. It is as if it
is left up to you to do that. Because you do know what your thorn is—
don't you? A thorn is pretty small, but it hurts so much. You have tried
so hard to make it better. You know you have so many blessings in life,
but you can't really enjoy them because, well, what about this thorn?

We are told that Paul's thorn didn't come from God, but from
Satan. It must have been something bad. So, surely, Paul thought, God
would remove it. Yet he didn't. Instead, what God told Paul was what
he tells us: "My grace is sufficient for you, for my power is made perfect in weakness." Grace is not made to order, but it is sufficient. It
does not get rid of all the pain. It seems to leave just enough to help us
remember that we need a Savior.

❧

A Redemptive Grace

I can will what is right, but I cannot do it.

Romans 7:18

Read Romans 7

Occasionally, someone will ask me when I'm going to preach on sin. The question always makes me want to ask, "Is there someone you would like to bring to church that day? Or are you troubled by your own sins?" In either case, it just makes me want to talk a lot more about the grace of God.

I find people don't need to be convinced that they are sinners. Most of us find that easy to believe. What is hard to believe is that we can be forgiven. That is why we keep trying to manage our sins on our own. Yet the only way we can manage sin is with more sin. The only escape is simply to confess our sin so we can at last be freed by the grace of God.

We live in a society that is so unaccustomed to grace that the church has to keep going over this concept time and time again. Nothing illustrates our confusion about grace better than those who want to hear more hammering on sin.

We cannot stop sinning just because we keep hearing we are sinners. If we are going to change, we will have to discover something more redemptive than feeling guilty. This is where God's grace comes in. It does what we cannot do for ourselves. It forgives, which is another way of saying it allows us to change. It can even make us love sinners.

❦

The Grace of a New Life

"No one can see the kingdom of God without being born from above."

John 3:3

READ JOHN 3:1-21

It is always interesting when someone on an airplane asks me what I do for a living. Upon finding out, the questioners will either get very nervous, or, if they find out I'm a Presbyterian minister, they may try to witness to me. Sometimes I'm asked, "Yes, that's fine, but are you born again?" Well, I think, there it is. I can either just say "yes" and get back to work, or I can try to get at exactly what we mean by this wonderful phrase—born again.

Although the term is used only once in Scripture, it has become something of a catchphrase that signals what kind of Christian a person is. If by being born again, we mean that we have joined the right group of Christians, we have made the same mistake as the Pharisees, Sadducees, and Zealots, who each tried to set boundaries on the kingdom of God.

Being born is a rather passive process. No one chooses to be born. Certainly, none of us were born because we were convinced we needed to be. Birth is simply a gift that we receive. Jesus used the image because it described beautifully how we receive the new life he was literally dying to give us. That life has come to us only because God so loves the world, including you. There is nothing you can do to make God love you more. There is nothing you can do to make him love you less. Once you've received that incredible grace, it is like, well, like being born again.

❦

Being Gracious Is Not Just Being Nice

"Woe to you when all speak well of you, for that is what their ancestors did to the false prophets."

Luke 6:26

READ LUKE 6:12-38

At our church, parishioners are frequently invited to conduct a ministry of grace. Yet being gracious is not the same thing as being nice. The grace God gives us is often very disruptive of our other plans for life. When God was gracious to Abraham, he was required to move his family from their settled life. When Paul received grace it ended his career as a Pharisee. In grace, Jesus expected the rich young ruler to give his wealth away. All of that was grace because it invited people to lose the lives they had built for themselves, in order to receive a better life that only God could give them. Yet that is not the kind of grace we want.

What we prefer is a nicer, more accepting grace that says, "Whatever you want is fine with God." However, if the purpose of grace is to save our lives, it is not gracious to accept just any behavior. Some things are wrong, and it is merciful to say so. In a day when the only absolute is to say there are no absolutes, that will not set well. If we would like to be popular, conducting a ministry of grace is the last thing we want to be doing. If we want to really love people, though, we will be committed more to their health than to our popularity. That doesn't mean we have to pass judgment on people. It does mean that we can help them depend on God.

❦

Living Under Heaven

Our citizenship is in heaven, and it is from there that we are expecting a Savior, the Lord Jesus Christ.

Philippians 3:20

READ PHILIPPIANS 3

According to a recent Gallup poll, the majority of Americans believe in a literal heaven. Most of the people surveyed said they expect it to be a continuation of life on earth but without the wars, disease, death, and other inconveniences that cramp their present pursuit of happiness.

If heaven is something that is simply waiting at the end of time, or at least at the end of our time, then it is easy to say we believe in it. Yet that isn't the real question that Scripture asks us. The real question is, "Do we live under heaven?"

The biblical perspective on heaven and earth is not linear, as if earth comes first, and then heaven. Rather, it is vertical, so that all humanity exists on the earth and under heaven. The reason this is important is that heaven is not just a place we go when we die. Heaven is also a place that gives meaning and order to the earth that sits beneath it.

In the words of the old preacher, P.T. Forsyth, "If within us, we find nothing over us, we will succumb to what is around us." In a world that is divorced from heaven, the only reality is what we see. The only relationships we have are with those who are still alive. It isn't enough. Those who live under heaven, by contrast, enjoy a world where grace is a frequent invader.

❦

Receiving Grace in Spite of Yourself

"I believe; help my unbelief!"

Mark 9:24

READ MARK 9:14-29

There is a believer and an unbeliever living under the skin of every Christian I know. We feel both the attraction of faith and the unyielding restraint of doubt. The confident words of the anthems, hymns, sermons, or creed may express a certainty we don't feel. Sometimes we would love to be a participant in worship, but we may feel more like a spectator who cannot pretend. Yet we are here! There is at least a part of us that believes, and it seems only honest to acknowledge that as well. Doubt always accompanies faith, refining it and making it clear.

What really plagues us is not the questions we have about the existence, power, and love of God. Those doubts are serious, but they don't cause us anxiety. What we really doubt is that God loves us. Can he forgive us—even when we haven't forgiven ourselves? The thing we don't doubt is that we are sinners. As one theologian said, "Sin may be the only objectively verifiable doctrine of the Christian faith."

When the Church proclaims the grace of God it does not mean that God will forgive us only if we can muster up the belief to come back to him. What it means is that in Jesus Christ he has come looking for us, and on the cross he found us. The real question isn't whether we believe in that grace, but whether we have received it.

❦
Finding Grace in Failure

Then Peter remembered what Jesus had said: "Before the cock crows, you will deny me three times." And he went out and wept bitterly.

Matthew 26:75

READ MATTHEW 26:69-75

Jean Vanier has claimed that Christians receive two very different calls. The first bids us to begin following Jesus. We respond by preparing ourselves to do wonderful things for the kingdom. For a while, anyone can be a Christian success story.

The second call comes later, when we realize we cannot fulfill our dreams of a heroic spirituality. Our earlier enthusiasms are turned into humility. In the first call, we are the Peter who leaves behind his fishing nets and boldly promises to stand by Jesus, no matter what. In the second, we are the disillusioned, faithless Peter, who sits by the campfire wondering why he denied Jesus.

We would like to believe that our resolve to do a good job as Christians will carry us through. Yet it never does. For all of us there has to come a moment, perhaps even a crisis, in which we realize that we can't pull off this business of being Christian. The marks of flawed humanity that we thought we left behind with the fishing nets have actually followed Jesus with us, reminding us why we need a Savior. As dark as that moment is, only then can we receive the second call—an invitation to live by God's grace. To live by grace is to come with empty hands to God. When our resolve is no longer in the way, God can transform us and use us greatly in the kingdom. Usually that is not in spite of our wounds, but through them. From then on, we are free to live all of life as an expression of gratitude.

❦

The Point of the Story

"This people's heart has grown dull."

Matthew 13:15

READ MATTHEW 13:10-15

There's nothing worse than telling a hilarious joke only to hear someone say, "I don't get it." When you have to explain the joke, it loses its punch. But those who discern the irony, twists, and double meanings in a story always burst out in delightful laughter. It also helps if you have a sense of humor, and for that you need a lively heart.

The parables of Jesus are like sacred jokes, with really important punch lines. They aren't jokes in the sense of being untrue, but they do have an ironic twist about them. The smallest mustard seed becomes the largest shrub. The wheat looks just like weeds until the harvest.

A man sells everything he has to buy a single pearl and thinks he got a great deal. When Jesus told these parables nobody ever seemed to "get it." Finally he said, "This people's heart has grown dull." The interesting thing is that he kept telling the parables anyway.

To this day, Jesus is still telling ironic parables about his grace in our lives. We lose our jobs only to discover the faithfulness of God. We become deathly sick and learn the meaning of life. We get married and then realize only God can cure our loneliness. If we're going to see the grace buried in the parable, we have to take care of our hearts. Those with dull hearts never see more than loss and hurt. Yet those whose hearts are alive with love for Jesus will find his grace in every story. Occasionally, they'll even break out in laughter.

❦

Remember God's Grace

So they committed themselves to the common good.

Nehemiah 2:18

READ NEHEMIAH 2

A hundred years after the Babylonians destroyed Jerusalem and carried the young people off into captivity, the people who remained in the city had become used to things being so bad. Yet when a Jew named Nehemiah came to visit Jerusalem for the first time, he was horrified. At one point he screamed out to the people, "Can't you see the trouble we are in?"

Actually, it is amazing how easy it is to stop seeing our problems in the city. Poverty-blindness is our favorite coping mechanism. When a homeless person does pierce through our defenses, we typically tell ourselves that they have made their bad choices, and then we hurry by.

The striking thing is that Nehemiah could still see the poverty. That was because he remembered "the hand of God had been gracious upon me." Grace is God's choice to give us what we need, not what we deserve. If you have received this grace, it makes you gracious. You're not so quick to tell people to take care of themselves, because you remember that the Savior took care of you. You're not so quick to rush by human need, because you are so thankful that the Savior did not rush by you.

After the people of Jerusalem remembered that they had received the grace of God, they were eager to invest in the common good. We, too, will invest in rebuilding our city only when we become thankful that God did not abandon us to our own bad choices.

❦

The Appearance of Grace

"Are you the one who is to come, or are we to wait for another?"
Matthew 11:2

READ MATTHEW 11:1-6

John the Baptist had devoted his life to getting people ready for the arrival of the Messiah. Yet once the long-awaited Savior arrived, most of the things he did came as a big surprise to John. It became immediately clear that Jesus was pretty loose about following the purity laws, and he was not at all careful about the people with whom he associated. Meanwhile, John had been put in jail for the hard line he had taken on King Herod's sin. As he heard more about Jesus' ministry, John became so confused that he sent some of his followers to ask Jesus if he really was the Savior.

I think John knew he was in trouble the moment Jesus asked to be baptized by him, because that act identified Jesus with our sinful lives. That had to be confusing to John, who had been warning people that when the Messiah came, he was going to bring a lot of fire and judgment with him. Instead, Jesus brought the possibility of forgiveness and a new life.

It may be that you, too, have been praying for a long time, asking Jesus to straighten out a bad situation. That is a dangerous prayer, because when Jesus straightens something out, it always happens differently than you had anticipated. Remember, if Jesus is the long-awaited one, then you cannot be the Savior. So the chances are good that Jesus will not use your plans for making changes.

❦

Justice Served, Grace Delivered

"Whom do you want me to release for you, Jesus Barabbas or Jesus who is called the Messiah?"

Matthew 27:17

READ MATTHEW 27:15-26

Barabbas' first name was also Jesus, which means "savior." So Pilate was presenting the crowd with two different saviors. One he would return to them, and the other he would crucify. Since Barabbas' guilt was so well known, Pilate thought this would insure the release of the other Jesus—the one "who is called the Messiah." Yet that illustrates how little Pilate knows about us.

We understand Barabbas, relate to him, and find ourselves in his life. Especially the part about his guilt. Barabbas wasn't all bad. Mark tells us that he was a revolutionary who was just trying to save the Hebrews by getting rid of the Romans. Yet one day during an insurrection he was leading, an innocent person was killed. That is the worst part of our guilt. Trying to do something good, we have hurt more than one person along the way. Parents understand this. So do spouses, friends, and colleagues. Even if the hurt happened long ago, we cannot escape the sentence of guilt.

Like Barabbas, we would love to be free from this guilt. Yet of course, that can happen only if Jesus takes our place on the cross. Barabbas couldn't just apologize for killing someone. Justice had to be served. We've always believed that. That's why we can't accept grace unless there is justice for what we have done. "Somebody has to pay!" Yes, and that is why Jesus the Messiah died for Barabbas' sins. And for yours. And for mine.

❦

Something to Talk About

"We cannot keep from speaking about what we have seen and heard."

Acts 4:20

READ ACTS 4:1-22

Clearly, God has called us to be his witnesses. Yet that can lead to two mistakes. The first is to try to be more than a witness and convert people to our faith. Only God converts people. Our calling is simply to be witnesses. The last thing a witness should do is to try to make something happen. Witnesses just talk about what they have seen and heard. So to be a witness at home, work, or in the world around us means nothing more than speaking about what we see God doing.

We sometimes say that the way we live is our witness. That's true, of course. Yet if we are living as people who are following Jesus Christ, we're going to be so strange that sooner or later, someone is going to ask us about our beliefs. Then we're going to have to do some talking.

The second mistake is to treat God's call to be a witness like an unwelcome subpoena. We're terrified of losing our friends who may feel judged by our witness. Yet we haven't been called to judge anyone. We've been asked to talk about the grace of Jesus Christ, who was judged for us. The apostles never thought about witnessing as something they had to do. They were so excited about what they had seen and heard, they couldn't help talking about it. So if you're having a hard time getting excited about being a witness, you may need to spend more time listening to God and watching the amazing things he is doing.

❦

Failure Is Breaking Even

"I was afraid, and I went and hid your talent in the ground. Here you have what is yours." But the master replied, "You wicked and lazy slave!"

Matthew 25:25-26

READ MATTHEW 25:14-30

Remember Jesus' parable of the master who gave money to his three servants? Two of them invested it, and they were praised. The third servant, however, did not receive as much as the others. He was afraid of losing what little he had, so he buried it in the ground. When the master returned, that servant gave the money back, proud that he had not taken risks with it. Yet to his surprise, he was judged harshly.

In the strange economy of God, failure is not the making of mistakes. Failure is breaking even. At no place in Scripture is anyone condemned for mistakes made while trying to contribute to God's work in the world, the coming kingdom of Christ. I take great comfort in knowing that God can always redeem our mistakes. However, we simply cannot take our lives and resources and hold on to them till the day we die, saying, "At least I broke even."

Life is short. The sooner we figure out how to use what we have for the kingdom, the more time we have to enjoy working with God. Certainly you have received some tangible signs of God's grace in your life. Whether they are great or small is not the issue. The issue is, will you be a good steward of this grace? Will you invest it in the risky business of the coming kingdom?

TWO

Never-Ending Mercy:
God's Love, Our Response

❦

God's Great Desire

You are precious in my sight, and honored, and I love you.

Isaiah 43:4

READ ISAIAH 43:1-4

What God wants, more than anything, is for us to love him. That is the beginning and the end of Scripture. We may have questions about his will for our future, our health, and our hard choices in life. Yet the Bible makes it perfectly clear that above all else the will of God is to be in love with us.

Often that isn't good enough. More than his love, what we really want is for God to help us out. Frequently, our relationship with God is characterized not by being in love, but by cutting good deals. We expect that if we are faithful in the Christian life, surely God will be faithful in taking care of the things we cannot take care of: he'll make sure our kids turn out OK, he'll cure the diseases that elude our medicine, and soon he will get around to fixing the world. Well, maybe.

If we could begin to focus our faith less on what God will do for us and more on God's great desire to love us, our lives would be revolutionized. First, people who are deeply in love tend to be less obsessive about things they cannot control. Second, we would discover that joy comes not from getting life fixed, but from knowing God. Joy is always born out of relationship. Third, we would be so transformed by receiving God's love that we could be of use to our lonely and frightened world.

29

❦

Into the Arms of God

If God is for us, who is against us?

Romans 8:31

Read Romans 8:28-39

Out of everything the Bible tells us about God, maybe the hardest to believe is that he is "for us." Some people wonder if God is out to get them. Yet most of us think God is neither for us nor against us. We assume he is too busy with international crises to be interested in our little lives.

The apostle Paul is very clear about this. God is for us, and that means he is for you also. Paul goes on to say that God gave up his own Son for us; there isn't anything that he has kept from us. Obviously, this doesn't mean that we receive everything we ask God to give us. No, it means that there isn't anything about God that he has held back from us. In giving us his Son, and his Spirit, God has revealed himself. He took the initiative. He said, "I love you" first. It's as though he were dying for a relationship.

In the second century, Irenaeus said that the Son and the Spirit are the right and left arms of God. He uses both to embrace us. Just as the father ran down the road to throw his arms around his Prodigal Son, so does the heavenly Father pull us into his heart with the ministry of his Son and Spirit.

People who have seen that have very little fear in their lives. If God is for us, who can be against us? So if you are still afraid, the trick is not to look at the things that threaten you, but at the arms that hold you.

Extravagance of God

O Lord, our sovereign ... what are human beings that you are mindful of them?

Psalm 8:1, 4

READ PSALM 8

I had been in seminary for less than a month when one of my professors quoted W.H. Auden in telling us, "Thank God your being is unnecessary." It was a hard message. We had all just begun a life of Christian service only to hear that not just our work but our very existence wasn't necessary.

For almost twenty years I have struggled with that quote. I understand that God and creation could get by without me, and that most everything I do could be done by someone else. "Yet surely we are all necessary," I keep thinking. Auden would say, "No. You are important, valued, and deeply loved—but not necessary." We all want that love more than anything else, but most of us feel more secure in being necessary.

All important things, Auden writes, are unnecessary. Art, music, joy, friendship, love, and peace are all unnecessary. If this is true, and I am still not completely convinced, then the only thing that can make life meaningful is if it is given value. We can value our lives, others certainly can as well, but all of this value is dependent on the only one who is necessary—our God who decided to love us.

It's amazing how easy it is to confuse being loved with being necessary. If God alone is necessary, if that is what it means to be God, then we are freed from settling for necessity when we yearn to be loved. (So, I guess, thank God our being is unnecessary.) It may be the only way we can believe that God and others have chosen to love us.

❦

How to Avoid Stress

Consider your own call, brothers and sisters: not many of you were wise by human standards, not many were powerful, not many were of noble birth.

1 Corinthians 1:26

READ 1 CORINTHIANS 1:18-31

One of the things I like about Washington, D.C., is that it doesn't really matter where you were before you got there. You don't have to have come from a respected family or possess a great deal of money. You just have to work hard. In fact, the more humble your origins, the more impressed people are by your success. So from the politicians on down to the lowly interns, a lot of us are compensating for our lack of noble birth with great ambition.

The church has never really cared much about pedigrees either. You can't arrive at the gates of heaven talking about your parents. The question then is going to be about your own relationship to God. Knowing that, many of us then assume that we have to work pretty hard to make it into God's kingdom, just as we have to do in our city. So we knock ourselves out, thinking we will impress God with all the personal achievements and good choices that we've made. Yet as Paul goes on to remind us, "God is the source of your life in Christ Jesus."

All that we have become is really a grace, an unmerited gift. Ultimately what matters are not our choices, but God's choice to love and bless us. After we receive that love, we can stop working to become somebody. Now, everything we do is just gratitude. We may still work hard, but without all of the stress. Grateful people are never stressed.

❦

Loved—Scratches and All

We have this treasure in earthen vessels.

2 Corinthians 4:7, RSV

READ 2 CORINTHIANS 4:7-18

My mother used to keep two very distinct sets of dishes. One set resided in the china cabinet. It was pretty special and would be brought out only when important people were coming to dinner. To be caught using the good china for a bowl of Wheaties was close to an unforgivable sin in our house.

For the family meals, we always went to the other set of dishes that were kept in the dish drain by the sink. They included a collection of Corelle Ware with three different patterns around the edges, a couple of plates on permanent loan from the church kitchen, and a wide assortment of scratched glasses bearing the names of the Empire State Building, McDonalds, and the Red Moon Pizzeria. Now, if you came over for dinner, and Mom set the table with the Corelle Ware, it meant you weren't too impressive as a guest. Yet it also meant you were considered family.

In trying to describe the Church, Paul compares it not to the good china but to "earthen vessels,"—early Church Corelle Ware, dishes that have been badly battered, but still contain the treasure of the gospel. If church history tells us anything, it's clear God has not treated us as fragile china. That's because he loves us too much. It's as if we were family, which of course we are. That's the treasure of the gospel. We can pull up to God's table anytime. We belong there, not because we're so impressive, but because we're loved—scratches and all.

❦

All for You

"My Father, if it is possible, let this cup pass from me; yet not what I want but what you want."

Matthew 26:39

READ MATTHEW 26:36-46

This was the essence of Jesus' prayer in the garden of Gethsemane just before he was arrested, tried, and crucified. We tend to emphasize the last part of this prayer, in which Jesus subordinates his wants for the will of his Father. Yet I wonder if we really understand the power of that until we remember that Jesus did not want to go to the cross. He had no martyr complex. While being fully God, Jesus was also fully human. He loved his life and did not want it to end horribly on a cross. That is why his submission to God is so overwhelming. He had to give up the life he so enjoyed. In fact, he even asked God to let this cup pass from him.

As far as we know, this is the only prayer by the Son of God that was denied. Not even Jesus could prevent God from giving us forgiveness. I wonder what was happening in the heart of God when he heard this prayer from his Son. Did it break in half? Did the heavenly Father break down and weep?

I am a parent. Like most fathers, I would do anything, absolutely anything, to insure the well-being of my child. It is one of the most important things in my life. What could possibly make the heavenly Father send his only Son to the cross? Nothing, except his love for us—also his beloved children.

No Ordinary Friend

The friendship of the Lord is for those who fear him.

Psalm 25:14

READ PSALM 25

I'm struck by how many of us strive to serve God as if his strongest attribute is anger. Perhaps this is because in our childhood we were exposed to a vision of God the Father that stressed how much he has done for us and how little we have done for him. Falling short, we were told, makes Daddy very angry. This vision has the effect of making all our service little more than a codependent effort at appeasing a father who is never satisfied, no matter how good we are. So we continue to be afraid of our angry God even as adults.

The Bible does call us to fear God—but not because of his anger nearly so much as his love and friendship.

The Creator, who made the heavens and the earth, is so passionate about us that, in Christ, he went even to the cross to find us. This is no ordinary friend we've got. He's going to be hard to control. He's not going to tell us what we want to hear, show up only when we want him, or be just another ornament in our neatly ordered lives. This friend is going to confront us with the truth and go with us to places we don't want him to be. He's going to give us his own passion for things we would rather avoid.

Hardest of all, God will enjoy us even when we're afraid we're not good enough to enjoy either him or ourselves.

❦

Unpredictable Mercy

"Do you want to be made well?"

John 5:6

Read John 5:1-18

Occasionally the water at the pool of Bethesda would get stirred up. According to legend, the first person to step in the pool afterward would be healed of whatever disease he or she had. One day as Jesus passed by, he noticed an invalid who had waited by this pool for thirty-eight years, trying to be healed. Yet since there was no one to help him, he was never first. Seeing the man, Jesus asked him the most striking question—Do you want to be made well?

It is hard to believe that anyone who is sick would not want to be made well. I know that some people can get used to their suffering, but no one enjoys having a body that hurts or doesn't work well. So why did Jesus ask that question? Perhaps it had something to do with the man's single devotion to the pool for his miracle. When confronted with the Savior Jesus, all he could do was complain about the problems he was having with his plans for healing.

We also have plans for making life better. We look to our work, money, exercise, and relationships as ways of improving the quality of our lives. When these plans don't work out, we can spend a lot of time complaining to Jesus. Perhaps we would do better to remember that it is a Savior to whom we are talking. Rather than insist that he use our plans to save us, we may have to simply cast ourselves upon his unpredictable mercy.

❦

Finding Your Significance

"Do you thank the slave for doing what was commanded?"
Luke 17:9

READ LUKE 17:7-10

I once had a teacher whose favorite expression was, "There is no reward for that which is expected." It was a hard lesson to learn as a child, but I'm glad old Mr. Blalock drilled it into me in the seventh grade. Apparently, though, some of us were sick the day they explained that at school, because a lot of people expect to be rewarded for doing what they are supposed to do.

We live in an age that is addicted to affirmation. If we do our jobs well and no one notices, we feel unloved and unimportant. Pretty soon we're thinking it's time to move our efforts to a different place where we will be appreciated. That is because we have made our joy dependent on the affirmation of others. Like any addiction, you can never get enough of this one. You constantly need more of the drug to get the same high. The only path to freedom is to find your significance from being in love with God. Work can never, ever, do that. It's just work. No matter how good your job is, or how successful you are at it, it's a really lousy lover. Yet when we are convinced that we are important to God who loves us, then we no longer have to ask too much of our work.

Joy in our labors is found not in the opinions of others, but from viewing work as an expression of gratitude to God. So we do what we ought to do, not so we will be loved, but so we can love God.

✤

Really Known, Really Loved

God proves his love for us in that while we still were sinners Christ died for us.

Romans 5:8

READ ROMANS 5:1-11

Recently a friend reminded me that there is nothing I can do to make God love me less, and there is nothing I can do to make him love me more. It is always the simple theological statements that are the most powerful. This one may be too powerful. It certainly takes away our leverage for manipulating God. He won't give us more attention if we just figure out how to really impress him. Of course this also means that the only one who knows all the secret, hard truths about us couldn't be more in love with us. That's the part that's too powerful.

Many of us assume God's love must be tied to something—our performance, our sacrificial service, or at least our ability to love him. Yet Scripture is rather clear about this. God's love is rooted only in his nature to be merciful. God really knows us and he really loves us. Usually we think we can have only one or the other. Since we want people to love us, we may be careful with how much we let them know. When we succumb to this temptation, we're sentenced to manipulating our relationships into what we think they should be.

When love is not volatile, when we have accepted the truth, we are allowed to conduct our relationships in freedom. It is the gracious love of God that introduces us to this freedom. According to Scripture, if we know about that grace, we will be less interested in fixing our loved ones and more committed to enjoying their love.

Tied Together for the Race

Run in such a way that you may win it.

1 Corinthians 9:24

READ 1 CORINTHIANS 9:24-27

The apostle Paul often compared the Christian life to running a race. Here he claims that the point of entering a race is to win. When you're halfway through the race, it isn't a good time to check your pulse, to ask others how you look, or to wonder why you entered the race. You need to remain focused on the finish line. It is the only way you can possibly win.

I would dare to add that not only is the Christian life like a race, it's like a three-legged race. Remember those crazy things? A kid ties a leg to another kid's leg, puts an arm around the other's shoulder, and then they hobble and trip their way toward the finish line, where they collapse in a fit of laughter. You probably won't see it in the Olympics. It tends to show up more often at church picnics. In fact, three-legged races were probably invented by the Church. It's one of our better metaphors.

We are tied to each other. That means we can't run as fast as we could if we were on our own. Yet it also means that we always have someone's arm around our shoulders.

All of Paul's inspired advice still applies. You run to win the race. You sure don't wonder about how you look. And you've got to stay focused on the goal. Yet at the end you aren't thinking about glory. That's because you're laughing too hard, which is what it means to win.

❦

God's Waiting Rooms

Do not fear, for I am with you.

Isaiah 43:5

Read Isaiah 43:5-10

Every time I enter a hospital waiting room, it feels as though I am walking into another dimension in time. The families who wait there, eager for some hopeful news about their loved one, are frequently tired and anxious. They pass the time doing what they can to help each other: telling stories, reading Scripture, praying, and reassuring each other. Yet mostly what everyone does in a waiting room is wait.

Of course, hospitals aren't the only places that make you wait. Some of us are waiting in relationships or employment. Others are waiting anxiously upon medical tests. Yet the report, or the phone call, won't come. "How long can it take?" we wonder. Longer still.

That is the context for what Isaiah has written. These words were given to the Hebrews who had spent a long time in exile waiting for God to take them home. This is not unlike our wait for Jesus Christ to bring about his kingdom of peace and justice. When we see the continued violence in the world, or even in our own streets, we wonder, "How much longer?" Longer still.

In the meantime, we do what helps in a waiting room. We take care of each other in this world. And we tell our stories. My favorite story, the gospel, reminds us that we don't need to fear because God is with us while we wait. Until the wait is over, our mission is to witness to God's presence in the world that he so loves.

*

Conquering Love

"Love your enemies and pray for those who persecute you."
Matthew 5:44

READ MATTHEW 5:43-48

One of the strangest things we are told is "Love your enemies." When someone falls in love with a sweetheart, we smile and say, "Good for you." When someone offers love to those who are the victims of oppression, we are impressed. It touches our hearts. Yet when someone loves the enemy, we get confused.

We knew Jesus wasn't going to tell us to hate our enemies, but we didn't expect we would be asked to love them either. Actually, we thought Jesus would say something like "Don't have enemies." However, the Gospels make it clear that Jesus himself had plenty of them. The Bible assumes that if we are living a life that is even half righteous, we are certainly going to have enemies who feel very threatened by the choices we are making. In fact, we can almost say that if we are keeping everyone happy, we haven't been following Jesus very closely. Enemies are a given in the Christian life. The question is, what do we do with them?

From the very first days of the Church, its greatest weapon has always been that the persecuted have offered love to the persecutor. The reason for this, as history has proven, is that it doesn't just confuse our enemies, it conquers them. Of course, the only people who understand this have themselves been conquered by the love of Jesus.

✤

Making the Impossible Possible

*May the Lord make you increase and abound in love for one
another and for all.*

1 Thessalonians 3:12

READ 1 THESSALONIANS 3:9-13

Have you ever tried to make yourself love someone? It's pretty hard.
We prefer to think of love as something magical that happens between
people who fall into it—as if love were a delightful gift for which we
are not responsible. So, loving someone just because we decide to isn't
easy. People who hurt us are particularly hard to love. It is one thing
for the Bible to ask us not to seek revenge on these people, but how
can it realistically ask us to love them? Other people are hard to love
because we just don't know them very well. I've never known what to
do when people I've just met smile and say, "I love you." Frankly, loving people we don't really know seems a little cheap. Yet Paul has asked
us to abound in love for one another and for all. How do we really love
everyone?

It seems impossible, and maybe that is exactly the point. There is no
human way we can love everyone. Yet with God all things are possible.
He can even change our hearts. If we want to become more loving, the
place to start is not by looking at our relationships but at our God, who
is love (see 1 Jn 4:8). He can fill our hearts with so much of his love that
it just keeps spilling over into everyone we meet. So maybe we're right.
Maybe love *is* a delightful gift for which we are not responsible.

❦

Going for Broke

Now the whole group of those who believed were of one heart and one soul.

Acts 4:32

READ ACTS 4:32-36

It is often asserted that people aren't interested in committed relationships anymore. However, I don't think that is true, or at least it isn't quite true. I think we are very interested in commitment. We just aren't very good at it.

For a long time our society has been preoccupied with the individual. We have trashed a lot of relationships, pursuing our own fulfillment. Yet this old preoccupation seems to be running out of steam. The divorce rate is now declining. Men's movements focused on keeping promises are quite popular. Corporations are not moving employees so often. Even television has returned to portraying healthy friendships. If nothing else, this indicates that we are yearning for committed relationships again. The question is, will we remember how to find them after ignoring them for so long?

When Luke described life in the early Church he said those who believed had one heart and one soul. That gives us a great clue as to how to find commitment. It says we don't find it. Rather, commitment finds us and binds our hearts and souls to others who share our beliefs. So commitment isn't really something we make; it's something we receive. If we want to receive it, the place to begin is with our beliefs. We'll have to give up believing our own happiness is most important and start giving ourselves to others with all the passion of Jesus Christ. We'll never be able to do that, however, until we first believe that Christ gave himself to us.

❦

Give More, Get More

The soul of Jonathan was knit to the soul of David.
1 Samuel 18:1, RSV

Read 1 Samuel 18:1-5

David and Jonathan did not spend a lot of time together. They came from very different backgrounds, had nothing in common, were on opposite sides of a civil war, and had no future together. Yet they became incredible friends.

They met right after David killed Goliath. We are told that "the soul of Jonathan was knit to the soul of David." The Hebrew here is in the passive voice, which means this was not something that they did, but something that happened to them. The best relationships often are not the ones we would have chosen, but they are the gifts we have received.

Let's not stop there, though. It is one thing to fall in love with those we hold close in daily life. It is another to care deeply about the pathos of the world. Most of us are kept pretty busy just trying to love family and friends. How can we also make room in our hearts for a teenager in the inner city or a frantic mother in an impoverished third world country?

One of the fascinating things about love is that it isn't quantitative. It isn't as though you only get so much, and then it's used up. To the contrary, the more you give, the more you receive, the more there is to give.

It still surprises me, but I know it is true. It is in giving our love away to the world that we find there is more to bring home.

❦

Not as Bad as You Might Think

"For God so loved the world ..."

John 3:16

READ JOHN 3:1-21

It is easy for the world to become the Church's enemy rather than the object of its compassion. Having been converted away from a journey in the wrong direction, most of us want to avoid the allure of the world's temptations to power and glory. However, to walk away from the world is also a journey in the wrong direction. It is certainly not a journey toward God.

Much of our inability to live at peace in the world is rooted in our misconceptions about God. We are so certain of God's anger and judgment, but so unsure of his mercy and compassion. When we radically distance God from his world, we are left with only the judgment that must be assumed by such distance.

When we recognize Christ at the office, in our neighbor's house, or in the shelters and missions, we cannot help but open our arms and embrace the world he died to love. We discover that the world is sanctified wherever he is present. This gives us the freedom to enjoy God's creation, as fallen and hurtful as it remains. As long as Christ can be seen, we have every reason in the world to be joyful and to live passionately in all of life's common places.

Maybe we need to speak of a second conversion. In this conversion, the heart repents of its resentment toward the world, and we turn back to the place from which we came, not as slaves but as lovers. Yet this second conversion cannot take place until we see God in the places from which we are running. Then, it is as if we were born again once more.

❦

Fearless Choice

Let your gentleness be known to everyone. The Lord is near.
Philippians 4:5

READ PHILIPPIANS 4:4-9

At a wedding I once attended, the groom inserted into his vows the statement that he would always be gentle to his bride. It was so unusual that everyone talked about it at the reception. Especially the married folks. Imagine always being gentle in your relationships. If that isn't hard enough, how about being gentle to the people at work?

Paul tells us to be known by everyone for our gentleness. Clearly he didn't live in Washington, D.C. No, but when he wrote this, he was imprisoned and suffering under Nero. This was his reward for spending so many years being chased with rocks out of most of the cities of Galatia and Greece. Actually, Paul knew more than we do about the cruelty of harsh cities. So it is ironic that he doesn't tell us to get tough. He tells us to be gentle.

Our difficulty with gentleness is rooted in our fear. We are afraid someone will take advantage of us if we are gentle. It has happened before. What's to prevent us from being run over again?

When I was a little kid, I didn't care much about the bully on the block if my big brother was near. Well, the Lord is near you, Paul says. If you can see that, you won't be afraid. So the degree to which you are known for your gentleness is the degree to which others will see, not your fear, but that Jesus is near.

The Lord Is With You

... the child conceived in her is from the Holy Spirit.
Matthew 1:20

READ MATTHEW 1:18-25

It must have been striking to Joseph and Mary that the angel gave them two different names for their son. The first name, *Jesus,* means Savior. The second, *Emmanuel,* means God with us. We don't usually think of salvation as having God with us. We would rather think of it as us being with God and being saved from how it is. However, in Jesus Christ, God is revealed as the Savior, Emmanuel, which means that salvation is not our ascent from the hard, pain-filled, compromised conditions of life. Salvation is God's descent to find the lost world he loves.

It follows that true spirituality for us must always exist within our ordinary, compromised, and ambiguous lives. In God's search to find us, he enters every dark and confused corner of life and sanctifies it simply by his presence. This means we can spend a lot less time praying for deliverance from how it is and a lot more time praying to see the face of God in every circumstance.

As Joseph and Mary demonstrated later in their life with Jesus, we can spend years with God in our families and not realize it. Yet when we do start to see that it is God who is with us, we can find life's meaning in the full range of human experiences, many of which are painful. So even for Christians there will be days of laughter and days of tears. In the words of the angel Gabriel, "The Lord is with you.... Do not be afraid."

❦

No Defense Against Love

Am I to come to you with a stick, or with love in a spirit of gentleness?

1 Corinthians 4:21

READ 1 CORINTHIANS 4:9-21

Paul was out of patience with the church in Corinth. While he was away, it had not accepted his strong leadership. Several "arrogant" Christians had created significant divisions that were threatening the church's spiritual vitality. It's hard to know which tool Paul wanted to use on them—the stick or the gentle love.

If Paul were coming to us, we would likely say that we preferred he bring his gentle love and leave the stick at home. Yet I wonder if that is true. Some of us seem to prefer the stick. Maybe that is because we are used to it. We've all taken plenty of beatings by those whose angry words have left us bruised and wounded. By now we have learned how to defend ourselves against the weapons people use. In fact, we have a stick or two of our own. Yet how do we defend ourselves against gentle love? That is why love is so powerful.

We face the same choice that confronted Paul. There are times when those around us become so infuriating that we can easily justify the stick. Our problem is not to justify the stick, but to determine its effectiveness. The reason Jesus called us to love even our enemies is not to make us morally superior, but to change the heart of the enemy. Until that happens, Christians have not fulfilled their mission.

❦

Unromantic Reality

What does the Lord require of you but to do justice, to love kindness, and to walk humbly with your God?

Micah 6:8

READ MICAH 6:3-8

I am amazed at how many of us maintain very high standards of justice in the world but do not treat people particularly well. It is not hard to believe in justice for the poor. It is not hard to believe in proclaiming God's grace around the world. What is hard is to do justice and mercy to those with whom we work and live and worship. Maybe that is because we can always romanticize the poor, especially if we don't know them, but it is hard to maintain illusions about people who are essentially family.

Actually, the Bible doesn't ask us to believe in justice and mercy. It asks us to do it. Do it at home and at work. Do it for anyone God brings across your path. Do it in the name of Jesus Christ.

Some of us have been called to missions in the inner city or in distant countries. All of us have been called to pray for these places and to commit our hearts to the coming of the kingdom all over the world. Yet until we learn how to do justice with the real people God has given to us, we don't have much to offer the world. That's because it is not until we try to do justice and mercy at home that we realize how impossible it is. Then we have to ask a Savior to change our hearts. It is only after we have learned to pray for a Savior that we can be of use to God's plans for the rest of the world.

❦

Home From the Crusades

"Those who are well have no need of a physician, but those who are sick."

Mark 2:17

Read Mark 2:13-17

There are many reasons why we hear so much about our "mission in life" at church. We each have gifts that have been given to us by God. Obviously, God had a reason for giving us these gifts, and it wasn't just for us to take care of ourselves. Our mission in life always involves the compassionate giving of our gifts to others. Yet there are other reasons to consider our mission. All around us, people are suffering under great burdens. Sometimes we see this suffering close enough to let our hearts break open. Then the Holy Spirit enters these open places and calls us to make a response. Another reason Christians are propelled into mission is that they are so thankful for what God has done in their lives, so amazed at the grace they have received from Jesus Christ, that they have to use their lives to communicate this grace to others.

When we look in the New Testament, though, it appears that the primary reason Christians have a mission in their lives is that they are simply committed to following Jesus—wherever he leads them. For too long they wandered through life on their own, trying one crusade after another, becoming more and more lost. When Jesus found them he promised to bring them back home to the Father. As they followed this Savior, they found that the journey back to God always seemed to travel through the places where others also needed the Savior.

Eternal Boasting

For what is our hope or joy or crown of boasting before our Lord Jesus at his coming? Is it not you? Yes, you are our glory and joy!

1 Thessalonians 2:19-20

READ 1 THESSALONIANS 2:13-20

Have you ever wondered what we will talk about in heaven? Of course, we'll spend eternity just expressing our gratitude to Jesus. Yet Paul indicates we will also be showing off a little. Our boasting isn't going to have anything to do with us. No, what will make us so proud will be each other. Mothers understand this easily.

Remember how much your mom embarrassed you by telling everyone all the wonderful things you had done? You couldn't get her to talk about herself, but she loved talking about you. Even if your achievements are really pretty ordinary, you just know that when you get to heaven, your mother will have them taped onto God's refrigerator. That's because you are her "crown of boasting." Well, get used to that. According to Paul, heaven is the place where you are presented as someone who is pretty special.

You and I know that it isn't our ordinary achievements that make us special. It's the sacrificial love we have received. The mother who gives her life away to raise a child is, at best, an imperfect symbol of the Savior who died to raise us to new life. If you really believe that, you can stop worrying about your own achievements and start delighting in someone else. Imagine what would happen if we all started boasting in others. It would bring a little bit of heaven into earth.

❦

The Unholy Holy

Lord,... you alone are holy.

Revelation 15:4

READ REVELATION 15:1-8

When the Bible speaks of holiness, it does not refer to the morality of people, but to an essential characteristic of God. Only God is holy. Some theologians have described holiness as the "godness" of God.

The only time the Bible ever calls anything or anyone else holy is when that thing or person bears God's mark. Thus, even when we are described as a "holy people," it is only because God has decided to be in our midst. Christians sometimes get confused about that, thinking that it is up to them to be holy, or at least to look like it. Yet Jesus made it clear that the harder people try to look holy, the less holy they become.

The only way for us to be holy is to open ourselves to the presence of God, who brings holiness with him. The only way to be open to God is to confess that on our own we've made an unholy mess of things. That is particularly true for us religious types, who have learned how to paste a thin veneer of spirituality over lives that are as messy as those of the non-Christians we know.

The only things that mark a Christian when it comes to holiness are the marks of the cross—where Jesus died so the sacred would no longer have to be set apart. The only response we can make to something like that is to make sure we aren't too set apart from other unholy folks who are also in need of mercy.

❦

All That You Can Be

For we are what he has made us, created in Christ Jesus for good works, which God prepared beforehand to be our way of life.

Ephesians 2:10

READ EPHESIANS 2:1-10

After a while you get tired of self-improvement programs. You stop trying new diets. You give up looking for the big business deal. You let the membership at the health club expire. Maybe you even stop trying to be a better follower of Christ. "I am what I am," you think, "and people are just going to have to accept that." Yet if your life is anything less than a reflection of Jesus Christ, then you're pretending to be something less than who you really are.

Our true identities are given to us by God. So when people say things like, "You'll have to get used to my bad temper because that's just who I am," they are not really telling the truth. Paul tells us that we are what God has made us, and God did not make us angry, hurt, or mean. God created us in Christ Jesus for good works. Paul didn't tell us that so that we would keep striving to improve ourselves. We can't re-create our lives. But God can. In Christ Jesus that is exactly what he is doing—turning you into a new creation.

The closer you draw to Jesus, the more you will notice wonderful changes in your life. It is not unlike the changes that happen to people who spend their lives in love. Over the years they shape and mold each other. Sometimes they even start to look like each other. That's because being in love, especially with Jesus, brings out the best in you.

❦

A Handle on Holiness

You shall be holy, for I the Lord your God am holy.
Leviticus 19:2

READ LEVITICUS 19:1-2

I wonder how many of us want a holy person for a best friend or a spouse? We may think it would make us feel inadequate. We can easily imagine Mother Teresa in Calcutta, but how many of us would like to take her with us to work? It's kind of hard to imagine. Yet the Bible doesn't ask us to be impressed by holiness. It tells us to be holy.

The way we become holy is not by trying harder to imitate the saints or to fulfill more godly expectations of ourselves. In fact, being holy has little to do with trying harder. It has everything to do with our image of God. A.W. Tozer said, "The most portentous thing about us is not what we may say or do, but what we conceive God to be like. For it is by the secret heart of the soul that we move toward our mental image of God." No one tried harder to be holy than the Pharisees, and yet they drove Jesus crazy. When we make holiness the goal, we are usually doing it only for ourselves. Yet when we fall more deeply in love with God, we find that we move closer to him. That is how Mother Teresa and all the saints became holy. Their lives are but reflections of the God they loved.

We all start out in life with the same potential. Where we end up has little to do with what we accomplish, and everything to do with whom we love.

❦

A Clear Heart

Mary ... sat at the Lord's feet and listened to his teaching. But Martha was distracted with much serving.

Luke 10:39-40, RSV

READ LUKE 10:38-42

Like most sisters, Mary and Martha were wired very differently. Martha was the industrious, hard worker who tried to please people by always doing a good job. No doubt, she always made her parents very proud. Mary, by contrast, was the child who constantly brought home stray animals, and as an adult she was probably drawn to stray men. Her parents probably loved and worried about Mary a great deal.

Most parents raise their children to act like Martha, but we hope they somehow keep the tender heart of Mary. We would like our kids to be very happy, but we don't know how to nurture happiness as we do achievement. Happiness is found in the heart, and that is what scares us the most about our children. How do we insure that they don't get in trouble, following their hearts?

Jesus makes it clear that it is actually Martha who is easily distracted. "Martha, Martha, you are anxious and troubled about many things; one thing is needful" (Lk 10:41-42, RSV). Our kids need most of all to know what the "one thing" is that they are after in life. The one thing is found not in many achievements but in their hearts. The other place they may be able to find it is in the hearts of their parents. But, of course, that assumes we as parents have a clear idea about the one thing that is needful in life. Maybe the way parents can help their kids the most is to be clear about their own hearts.

❦

The Neighborhood of Christ

And who is my neighbor?

Luke 10:29

Read Luke 10:25-37

A lawyer once asked Jesus what he had to do to inherit eternal life. Jesus responded by asking him what was written in the law. The lawyer quoted a text about loving God and your neighbor as yourself. Jesus said, "See, you knew the answer. Do this, and you will live." Yet the lawyer then asked, "And who is my neighbor?" I would have expected Jesus to roll his eyes at this pathetic effort to find a loophole. Instead, he told the wonderful story of the Good Samaritan.

A man fell among robbers who beat him and left him barely alive. A priest and a Levite, two respected leaders, walked right by the man. When a Samaritan came by, he stopped, bound the wounds, and carried the man to safety. Samaritans were not respected. In fact, they were despised. After finishing the parable, Jesus asked, "Who was the neighbor to this man?"

Notice the important shift. The lawyer's clever question, "Who is my neighbor?" had been taken away from him and put into the mouth of the man lying on the side of the road. Who was his neighbor? Who lives next to him? Who identifies with this despised person in need of mercy? The lawyer responded, "The one who showed mercy." Right. In the neighborhood of Christ, there are only those who need mercy and those who give it. Actually, they are the same people.

It always comes back to receiving and giving mercy. Yet you knew that. Do it, and you will live.

THREE

God With Us:
Always Faithful, Always at Work

❦

It's Life, Not the Olympics

God created humankind in his image.

Genesis 1:27

READ GENESIS 1:26-31

It is the pastor's great privilege to witness a very fragile process that has to do with the unfinished nature of human lives. As people of faith quietly make their way through the ambiguity of daily life, they carry the creativity of God's Spirit with them. To watch Christians is to see a miracle slowly unfold. The miracle is this—they are accepting the mystery of their lives.

Many of us have been taught to live between the twin agonies of high standards and our nagging self-doubts. We have extraordinarily high goals, and we fail at them all the time. There is nothing for which we need salvation more than our attempts at being our own creators.

When we discover we have a Creator who isn't nearly finished with our lives, but has become involved in our failure and success, our joy and sorrow, we discover our lives are not our own. We are then converted from being the achievers with regret to the pilgrims with wonder.

None of that can happen unless our image of God is also converted. He is not the disappointed standard giver. He is our gracious Creator who is still at work.

❦

We Lift Our Eyes to the Lord

Lead me to the rock that is higher than I.

Psalm 61:2

Read Psalm 61

Sooner or later everyone is overwhelmed by a storm. Often the storm first hits your family, or your health, or your work. Yet then it moves around to create havoc in the other areas of life. Your child is critically ill, so you can't concentrate on work and it shows. Or your work is so stressful that you spend too much time in the office, and as a result your relationships are now stressed as well. Or the loneliness you feel in your personal life makes you look for community and intimacy at work. Yet work can never be more than work.

When a storm hits, we don't think about anything but getting help for the part of life that is in crisis. So we either ignore the other areas of life, or we rush to them for salvation. Both plans result only in spreading the storm around. That's when we feel overwhelmed.

We know that we ought to lift our eyes up to the Lord, who alone can be our Savior, but that is so hard. When a storm hits, our first reaction is always to put our heads down and run as fast as we can. We always discover, though, that the storm just keeps chasing us.

As the psalmist tells us, our only real hope is to pray to be led to the higher rock where we can get a glimpse of God's perspective on our problems. What we will see is that he is already at work, stilling the storm.

❦

Salvation in Thick Darkness

The people stood at a distance, while Moses drew near to the thick darkness where God was.

Exodus 20:21

READ EXODUS 20:18-26

Throughout their journey in the wilderness the Hebrews struggled with fear. They were afraid they were heading in the wrong direction. Then they were afraid they were going to die of thirst. Then of hunger. Then boredom. Yet most of all, the Hebrews were afraid of God.

When God gave Moses the Ten Commandments on Mount Sinai, it was clear to the people below that something big was happening up there. There was thunder, lightning, smoke, and worst of all, "thick darkness." We can handle thunderstorms in the daylight. It's the ones at night that are terrifying. So, it's no wonder the people kept away from the dark place where God was.

We prefer a kinder, gentler God who will lead us away from the dark, frightening places. Yet the places where our Savior finds us are always in the midst of the thick darkness. Remember how dark it was when the Savior was born? And when he died on Good Friday? Remember how few people were there? Most of us miss the Savior because we flee the dark places where he can be found.

Your journey through life is also interrupted with moments of thick darkness. They are the terrifying places where God is waiting for you. If you insist on running from them, don't be surprised if the rest of the journey is spent missing God.

❦

The Better Place

The Lord has proclaimed to the end of the earth ... "You shall be called 'Sought Out.'"

Isaiah 62:11-12

READ ISAIAH 62:6-12

Well, it's a new millennium, and we are still here. Will the Lord Jesus Christ delay another thousand years before coming back? Maybe. Maybe even longer. Yet as Jesus kept explaining during his last sojourn through earth, it just isn't up to us to know, or even guess, how long the in-between time will last. Two thousand years seem like a very long time to us, but from the perspective of eternity it's a blink of the eye.

Your calling is not to figure out the end of time, but to be good stewards of your days while you have them. That doesn't just mean you have to work hard and seek the completion of your goals. More importantly, it means you have to learn how to receive the God whose goal is to seek for you.

According to Isaiah, God's intimate, special name for you is Sought Out. He can't wait to find you tomorrow, so he has broken into today, searching for more of you than you may want him to find. There is nothing that can blind you to God's presence quite like thinking of today as only in-between time. That reduces the day to an obstacle that must be overcome on your way to a better place. Yet the better place is where the Lord is, and he is found only in the present that you are rushing by. Don't worry if you miss him, though. He'll keep looking for you, Isaiah promises, till the end of the earth.

❦

Riding Around in Sheol

Out of the belly of Sheol I cried, and you heard my voice.
Jonah 2:2

READ JONAH 2:1-11

To avoid the mission God had given him in Nineveh, Jonah tried sailing to Tarshish. Yet God has his own unique ways of getting us where he wants us to be. So Jonah got to ride back to Nineveh inside the belly of a great fish. The three days he spent in that fish did wonderful things for his prayer life, which may have been more important to God than getting Jonah to the right place.

It is easy to get lost in the critical debates about whether or not this story really happened, but that misses the point of the Scripture. Sure, I think it could have happened. God can do whatever he wants. The real question, though, is not whether it did happen, but whether it does happen. Do people still start off in one direction, then get swallowed up in something awful, only to discover that the crisis has actually brought them to the right place with God? You bet that happens. I see it all the time.

Sooner or later, we all spend time in the belly of Sheol. It's the place where you thought you were going to die, or maybe even the place where you wished you would die. It's so dark there that you can't find any reason to keep hoping.

Now you are at the hardest part of this story to believe. Is God really using this for good? Absolutely. Your ability to see that, however, will depend completely on your prayer life while you're riding around in Sheol.

❦

The Miraculous Mundane

"The kingdom of God is not coming with things that can be observed.... The kingdom of God is among you."
Luke 17:20-21

Read Luke 17:20-37

Wouldn't it be wonderful if God did something big in your life? I mean really big, so you would clearly know that you had just been visited by God. Maybe he would leave you healed of that which is incurable. Or maybe one day you would hear him speak to you in an audible voice. As shocking as it would be to have a bright light blind us like it did Paul, there isn't one of us who wouldn't love to have been with Paul when God grabbed hold of him. Just once, couldn't God do something spectacular in our lives also?

It could be that the yearning to have something miraculous happen is symptomatic of how hard a time we have in finding God in the common moments of life. Yet in claiming that God became flesh and dwelt among us, Scripture indicates that God will be found in the ordinary and even the mundane routines of life. The question is not whether God speaks to us, but whether we hear him. Have we become too distracted by the noisy routines of life?

Rather than waiting for God to do big things in your life, think about how God is finding you through the marvelously mundane moments of everyday life. For if the momentary is not sacred to you, then neither will be the momentous. Yet if the common moments of life are sacred opportunities for encountering God, then all of life will become rather spectacular.

❦

Life Interrupted

When Elizabeth heard Mary's greeting, the child leaped in her womb.

Luke 1:41

READ LUKE 1:39-45

They made an interesting pair. Elizabeth was "getting on in years" when she became pregnant with a boy who would become John the Baptist, her first pregnancy after many years of trying to have a child with her husband. By contrast, her young cousin Mary assumed she would need to have a husband before she started having babies. So it was too late for Elizabeth to have a child and too early for Mary. Unless, of course, you are God, in which case these pregnancies make perfect sense.

After the angel Gabriel announced God's miraculous intervention in Mary's life, he told her about the sacred interruption of Elizabeth's life. It's not surprising, then, that the Virgin headed straight to her cousin's home. In coming together, they formed the first community of Christ because they were two people gathered in his name (three, if you count John, who leaped up in Elizabeth's womb because he was so excited about the coming Savior). Much later, Jesus would say that whenever two or three were gathered in his name, he would always be in their midst.

To this day, whenever the community of Christ gathers, it is as a community of interrupted lives. Some of us, like Elizabeth, have discovered life isn't what we had settled for. Others, like Mary, have discovered life isn't what we had hoped for. All of us have discovered that when a Savior is in our midst, life isn't limited by our despair or our hopes.

❦

Right Here, Right Now

It is for you, O Lord, that I wait.

Psalm 38:15

READ PSALM 38

None of us is very good at waiting, but we all have to do a lot of it. We wait while standing in lines and sitting in traffic. We wait in waiting rooms cluttered with old magazines and at airport gates cluttered with weary travelers. We wonder if we'll ever get where we are going.

We also sometimes have to wait for news about something very important. Did you get into college? Do you have cancer? Will he ask you to marry him? You'll have to wait and see.

The most dangerous kind of waiting is when we expect life to begin in the future. Having judged today to be inadequate, we think we'll be happy if only we can get to our dreams. Yet when we do get there, we discover that hasn't made us happy either. So we develop a new dream. Again we say, if only we can get there, we'll be satisfied.

Nothing is more addictive than saying, "If only." Like any addiction, this one will suck your life away. If you are counting on tomorrow for your happiness, eventually you'll find yourself in a nursing home, saying, "If only I hadn't run past so many blessings, trying to get to the future."

Whether we realize it or not, what we are always waiting for is the presence of the Lord. The wonderful news of the gospel is that he can be found in every type of waiting room. However, you'll have to stop looking for him in the future in order to find him in the day you have.

❦

Give It a Rest

"Be still, and know that I am God!"

Psalm 46:10

READ PSALM 46

One of the hardest things for us to accept is that we have a God whose ways are not our ways. For this reason the Hebrews were once tempted to have "a god like the other nations of wood and stone" that would be predictable and familiar. It is for this same reason that today we turn to the gods of power and wealth, because we understand these idols. They expect us to work hard to contribute to our own salvation.

Any time we think we can find salvation from our hard work, we are in grave danger. If our hard work fails, or worse yet if it succeeds, then we are stuck with ourselves for a god. That means we have destined ourselves to journeying through life's wilderness assuming that the solution to every problem is to try harder.

People who live life without a Savior do not have any sense of awe or wonder. Nothing amazes or astonishes or overwhelms them because their world is too small for God to fit into. That is an awfully sad world that, unfortunately, has become quite crowded today. Yet I have discovered over and over again that God loves us too much to abandon us to that. He will come looking for us, as he did the Hebrews in slavery, and when he finds us, he will free us from anything that has bound us—even our success.

❦

The Challenge of the Familiar

God saw everything that he had made, and indeed, it was very good.

Genesis 1:31

READ GENESIS 1:1-31

When I was in a college art appreciation class, I wrote a paper on the paintings of Sir Joshua Reynolds. I had spent a lot of time in the museum and had studied his work thoroughly, so I wanted to demonstrate my expertise to the professor. I filled the research paper with references to the mistakes Reynolds had made in his portraits, the scratches that authenticated the original works, and the "obvious" ways he had used his students to paint the backgrounds of his portraits. When the professor returned my paper, her only comment was, "But what did you think of his art?"

It is so easy to discount the familiar, and to lose sight of the mystery and genius of that which we think we know so well. It is particularly hard to appreciate God's creativity in our own lives, because we get so used to the scratches that we can't see the art. This is often a challenge in relationships, and it is always a challenge when we look in the mirror.

Any novice can discover the flaws in something without much difficulty. That comes from spending too much time looking too closely at unimportant issues. It takes someone with vision, with an eye for the creativity of God, to see that the scratches have only made the art more treasured over time.

God has created you, and called you good. Jesus Christ died to save you, that God's good work may be carried to completion (see Phil 1:6). Yet it may take a while to see that.

❦

Surviving the Curves

Consider the work of God; who can make straight what he has made crooked?

Ecclesiastes 7:13

READ ECCLESIASTES 7:13-14

We are a people who like straight lines. We want our careers to take a straight line from the bottom to the top, our relationships to move consistently from good to better, and our lifestyles to just keep improving. Yet that never happens.

It is only a matter of time until every journey through life hits a major curve in the road. That's dangerous only when you're moving too fast to handle it. If you're paying attention to your life, when the curves come you won't insist on continuing to head straight for your goals, because that would run you into the ditch. No, the only way to survive a curve is to turn into it. The lost jobs, relationships, and dreams don't have to be the end of your life. They can simply be an invitation to start moving in a new direction.

The life you are living in the present is not what you were planning in the past. Isn't that good news? Can you imagine how dull your life would have been if you had stayed on a straight course toward all the goals you used to cherish? If you have ever driven on a road that runs in a straight line for miles and miles, you know how boring it can be. It's the curves that make a road interesting.

Remember, God designed the path you are traveling. If it has a curve in it, that is only because you will never get to his future filled with hope by continuing in a straight line.

❦

Trouble Enjoying God

All things came into being through him.

John 1:3

READ JOHN 1:1-18

It would be a mistake to think of Jesus Christ as "Plan B." We sometimes tell the gospel story as if God's first idea was for people to climb their way up into heaven by the Law, and when that didn't work out so well, he decided to send his Son to come and get us. Yet that is not what the Bible tells us. From the beginning, we are told, the Son was at work with the Father.

The same thing is true with your life. The Savior has also been involved in your life from day one. He was at work before you knew you needed salvation. He was at work in the good days and in the awful days. He was even at work when you couldn't see him because you were busy making big mistakes. Day after day, Jesus has been ever so subtly revealing God's salvation of your life.

So, although we sometimes encourage people to "invite Jesus into your life," I'm not sure that is consistent with John's Gospel. I think it is more accurate to say that Jesus invites us into his life with the Father. As we accept this invitation and believe in it, we can enjoy all the love the Father gave to the Son. From the beginning, after glorifying God, enjoying him is the reason we were created. So if you're having trouble enjoying God these days, maybe you just need to go back to the beginning and remember all the ways a loving Savior has been at work in your life.

❦

A Resting Place Along the Way

Then they came to Elim, where there were twelve springs of water.

Exodus 15:27

READ EXODUS 15:22-27

After the Hebrews had safely passed through the parted waters of the Red Sea, Moses was so grateful he broke out in song. Then his sister Miriam grabbed a tambourine and got all the women dancing and singing songs of praise and thanksgiving. It was revival time!

The road to the Promised Land that went along the Mediterranean coast was called "The Highway of the Philistines." It was the easy way. Yet God led them south, down into the desert, where the way is hard. Three days after the miraculous Red Sea crossing, the people arrived at Marah, where the water was bitter. They were out of resources, out of patience, and convinced they were heading in the wrong direction. That is pretty typical for anyone who is following God's direction. It was then that they received their first lesson on God's faithfulness. He broke into the Hebrews' complaints and said, "I am the God who heals you." That is usually why we are in the wilderness: to have our frightened hearts healed.

Then God led the people to a beautiful oasis called Elim where there was so much water they could play in it. After every Marah there is an Elim, a resting place for both body and soul. That is also revival time. Yet you never want to mistake Elim for the Promised Land. The purpose of an oasis is just to renew you enough to keep following God through the desert.

❦

Hitting the Road

Jesus Christ is the same yesterday and today and forever.
                                                        Hebrews 13:8

READ HEBREWS 13:1-8

My father was a church planter. For the first several years, his fledgling congregation met in the basement of a home. After years of saving, we bought a piece of property and moved a little white-frame church that had gone out of business onto it. I'll never forget seeing that old building, so precariously perched on a truck chassis, as it came wobbling down the street.

I loved the old white church. It was a place where a lot of folks for the first time heard the gospel my father preached. It was also the place where I first held the hand of the cute redhead who, years later, agreed to become my wife. So many memories.

Eventually the small white church gave way to a brand-new, big, brick building. Those of us who cherished the old church said things would never be the same. We had said the same thing when the congregation had moved out of the house into the white church. It's amazing how selective memory is. Few people remembered how angry they had gotten in the house when the youth group was singing "Do Lord" while the Ladies' Bible Study was trying to pray in the next room.

There are no good old days. There aren't necessarily even better future days. There are just the days we have, in which we confront more opportunities than we realize. Yet opportunity comes at a cost. If any church is going to survive, it has to hit the road.

Jesus is the same yesterday, today, and forever. Everything else is likely to change.

❦

A Friend in Jesus

"I do not call you servants any longer,... but I have called you friends."

John 15:15

READ JOHN 15:1-17

We don't tend to think of Jesus as having friends, and we sure don't consider the disciples his friends. We think of them more as his bumbling students who could never understand exactly what Jesus was saying. Yet shortly before Jesus was arrested and crucified, he looked at the disciples and called them his friends.

I wonder what was going on in their minds. Were they surprised? Were they honored? My guess is that they were again confused. We regard friends as our peers, and although the disciples loved Jesus, they knew they were hardly his peers. Maybe it confuses you, too, to think that Jesus would look at you one day and say, "friend."

What is it that makes you Jesus' friend? Obviously it involves more than serving his kingdom. Servants simply fulfill a job. They don't strive to understand the mind of the master, and they sure don't have to maintain a loving relationship with him. They just try to get the job done. Perhaps you would prefer to just remain a servant. It is easier, clearer, and less demanding. Yet as confusing as it is, only the friends of Jesus find relief for the deep spiritual loneliness inside them.

Maybe the thing that is hardest to believe is that Jesus is dying to have a personal relationship with you. You're never going to be his friend, however, until you believe that.

❦

Foolish Questions

"What are you looking for?"

John 1:38

Read John 1:35-39

One day John the Baptist pointed to Jesus Christ and said, "Look, here is the Lamb of God." Two of John's disciples left him that day and immediately began to follow Jesus. When Jesus realized they were walking behind him, he turned and asked them, "What are you looking for?" That is such a good question.

I can envision these two new disciples with their heads down, nudging each other to answer Jesus' question. Finally one of them said, "Teacher, where are you staying?" I'm thinking that the other guy put his face in his hands at this point. What a dumb response. Why didn't he say that they were looking for truth, or maybe the kingdom of God? Sometimes I wonder if the questions I ask God are really all that profound. I would love to impress God with all my speculations about the inner dynamics of the Trinity, but I'm not actually up all night thinking about that. The things that keep me up nights are much more trivial.

The fascinating thing about this passage is that Jesus took their question seriously, and invited the two men to follow him home. There they stayed with him, probably talking about a lot of other ordinary things. The important thing is not what they discussed, but with whom they were talking. There are no dumb questions you can ask Jesus. There aren't any smart ones either. Frankly, it doesn't matter what we ask. Jesus will still use the question to reveal more of himself to us. We need him a lot more than we need answers to our questions.

❦

Nothing Is Wasted

We know all things work together for good for those who love God, who are called according to his purpose.

Romans 8:28

READ ROMANS 8:28-39

These days, the currency we value the most is time. We cannot get enough of it. With the passing of another year it is easy to get even more worried about our time commitments, asking ourselves if we are accomplishing enough in the little time we have left. The last thing we want to do is to waste time.

As Christians we believe that each day is given to us by God, so we want to be good stewards of the gift of time. However, the Bible makes it very clear that God is always at work within us to bring about a good creation.

Scripture is full of illustrations of people who thought they were wasting time, only to discover later that God had a use for those experiences. If Moses had not spent forty years in the wilderness as a shepherd, he would never have known how to lead the Hebrews to the Promised Land. David spent a lot of time with a flock of sheep before he took over the flock of God. Paul's background as a Pharisee was quite useful when dealing with the Jewish-Christian disputes in the early Church. Even Jesus spent a lot more time as a carpenter than he did in his ministry.

If we give our lives over to God, he can use our past, our failures, and the time we spent chasing dreams that did not work out. That is what it means to have a Savior. Nothing is wasted.

꽃

Dodging Disaster

Because the Lord your God is a merciful God, he will neither abandon you nor destroy you; he will not forget the covenant with your ancestors that he swore to them.

Deuteronomy 4:31

READ DEUTERONOMY 4:25-31

Fifteen hundred years before the birth of Christ, Moses gave the Hebrews one last sermon before they entered the Promised Land. In this sermon, he predicted that even though the people had seen so many signs of God's faithfulness, they would still put their trust in idols after entering the land. Moses claimed that this would result in most of them being scattered, and others being led into captivity. There, he said, you will again "serve other gods made by human hands." All of those predictions came true. In the year 721 B.C. the ten northern tribes of Israel were defeated, dispersed, and never heard of again. In 586 B.C. the two southern tribes were carried to Babylon. They worshiped idols before these disasters, and they worshiped them afterward.

Not all disasters are a result of sin. Clearly, though, some are. As a pastor, I have found that when people make big mistakes, they often turn to the same idols that got them into trouble in the first place. Of course, that just leads to more disaster. What is most significant about Moses' prophecy is that he ends it by saying God will still save the people, not because we will eventually turn back to him, but because he has turned to us. Out of mercy, God will never abandon us, and he will someday bring us back to the Promised Land. There is nothing we can do to prevent a God who is determined to save us. Allelujah.

❦

Living With a Creator

In the beginning God created ...

Genesis 1:1, RSV

READ GENESIS 1:1-31

Any number of times I have felt like a failure as a father, but never so predictably as when I have encountered the words "some assembly required." More than once, I have gone home from Christmas Eve worship to do some assembly on a bicycle and found myself saying words that are not in the Christmas story. I often remember that scene when people come to see me because they are having difficulty getting life assembled just right.

Most of us look at our lives as if they come with a lot of missing parts, confusing instructions, and a pressing deadline to get it all together. Yet the Bible makes it clear that God alone is the Creator of our lives. From the beginning to the end of the biblical story, we discover not complex directions, but the high drama of a God who insists on doing all the assembly of our lives.

We sometimes refer to our work in life as a way of making a living. What a terrible term for mere creatures to use! Only the Creator can make a living being. Our calling is to receive the life that he is giving us, day by day, as he puts the pieces together.

So you begin each new day confronted with a great choice. You can try to achieve your life, but your constant companion will be complaint because you will never have achieved enough. Or you can choose to receive a life. Then your companion through the day will be gratitude for all the blessings God keeps giving you.

FOUR

The Choices We Make

❧

Who Is Your God?

"How long will you go limping with two different opinions? If the Lord is God, follow him; but if Baal, then follow him."

1 Kings 18:21

READ 1 KINGS 18:1-46

The Bible constantly confronts us with a choice. The thing that drives us crazy is that it isn't the choice we want. We prefer to choose our future, our relationships, our vocation, our lifestyle, and how we spend our money. Yet the Bible claims all of that depends on the one choice you have to make first—namely, who is your God?

We can choose ourselves for a god. Knowing what we know about ourselves, that would be an unfortunate choice, but it is amazing how many times we make it. We don't call ourselves gods; we just choose to act like them on the decisions that are important to us. The pursuit of power and wealth is another possible choice. Those gods will be hard to satisfy, but a great many of us dedicate our lives to serving them.

The hardest part about choosing to follow the God of the Bible is that we don't know where it will end. The promise is that he will lead us to salvation, but usually that doesn't look like anything we had imagined. That's why it's tempting to choose another god from time to time. Yet as the Bible says over and over, no one can serve two lords. They will lead you in opposite directions. To try to follow both is confusing and, frankly, exhausting. You'll have to make the choice. You can't keep limping between two opinions.

❦

Time to Make a Choice

"Lazarus, come out!"

John 11:43

Read John 11:1-44

If you have been to Israel, the chances are good that you have walked down into Lazarus' tomb. It's a dark, dark place. Actually, even if you've never been to Israel, you have probably been in that tomb at some point in your life. Maybe it was when you lost your job. Or when the doctor tried to explain about finding more of the disease. Or when someone you loved broke your heart. Yeah, you know exactly what Lazarus' dark tomb looks like.

The question is, once you get in there how can you still see the Savior? It's pretty hard when you're in a tomb. When life goes dark, you can't really see anything, including Jesus. That is when you have to trust your ears, and believe the words you hear proclaimed by the Church. Standing at the door of your tomb, Jesus calls you by name: "Lazarus, come forth!" Come out of your fear and grief and anger. Come forth from the dark place where you've been nurturing all that hurt. You don't have to be a victim. Why are you settling for this?

Now, you've got to make a choice. Are you going to believe there is a new life waiting out there, or are you going to settle into the place of death? Maybe you don't think you have that much belief. Maybe you can't see your way out of your grief or hurt just yet. Well, maybe, but do not wait for the faith to come, because there is little power in our faith. No, the power is in the Savior who is calling for you.

❦

Victimized or Victorious?

"God has made me fruitful in the land of my misfortune."
Genesis 41:52

READ GENESIS 41:1-52

If Joseph were alive today, he could be a poster boy for victimization. He was abused by his family, who sold him as a slave in Egypt. He tried to be a good slave to his master, but the master's wife threw him into prison when he wouldn't sleep with her. He tried to be a helpful prisoner, but all who regained their freedom still forgot about him. Joseph kept doing the right and honorable thing, and for his efforts he sank lower and lower, until at last he was abandoned to a dark corner of an Egyptian jail. It was all so unjust. Yet Joseph never thought of himself as a victim.

Victimization is quite in vogue in our society. We insist that we have been deeply hurt by our families, our supervisors, and our culture. "I deserve better than I have gotten," we demand. Maybe that's true. Yet it really doesn't matter what you deserve. What matters is how you respond to your hurt. You can settle into a deep anger that will suck away the rest of your life. Or you can choose to look for the ways in which God is molding your life even through injustice.

God cares a lot more about your character than your accomplishments. When he was young, Joseph had great dreams but little humility. After he was pulled out of jail, he was a different man. That's because he believed God could use even evil for good. Yet that took a choice. Victimization is the other choice. It is a choice to waste your suffering.

❦

Love: An Act of Will

"If you love me, you will keep my commandments."
John 14:15

Read John 14:15-24

We love to use the word *love*. Yet we prefer a nebulous understanding of it. When we find the courage to tell someone "I love you," we hope he or she doesn't ask us to explain exactly what we mean. That would really spoil the mood. No, all we want to hear is, "I love you, too." Then we can simply enjoy the romance of the moment.

If this is a serious relationship, however, we will eventually have to get specific about what we mean when we claim to be in love. That's when we start talking about commitments, responsibilities, trust, and sacrifice. And that is when we get scared.

Jesus never settles for our nebulous reassurances that we love him. The Bible indicates that he always pushes for a very specific understanding of what it means to love him. Sometimes it means leaving everything behind to follow him. Other times it means feeding his sheep. In this text, it means obeying his commandments. Yet the Bible never indicates that Jesus asks us to feel sentimental about him. In fact, he doesn't ask us to feel anything. He asks instead for a love defined by choices, faithfulness, and acts of the will. And again, that is when we get scared.

It is actually quite hard to love anyone, in any definitive sense, unless you have been loved. It is impossible to choose to love Jesus sacrificially unless you have received his love for you. His love, remember, was so passionate that he sacrificed his life on a cross for you.

❦

Redeeming Our Choices

"As for the son of the slave woman, I will make a nation of him also."

Genesis 21:13

READ GENESIS 21:1-20

When Sarah couldn't get pregnant, it was her idea for Abraham to try to have a child by Hagar, her slave. As soon as Hagar got pregnant, though, she also got a bit too haughty for Sarah's liking. So Sarah chased Hagar out into the desert, where an angel found her and brought her back home. Then Hagar gave birth to Ishmael.

A little later Sarah did get pregnant and gave birth to Isaac. Yet when she saw Ishmael playing with her little boy, Isaac, her old jealousy was inflamed. Again, she tried to make the problem go away. Again, God had to rescue Hagar and Ishmael in the desert.

It is fascinating that God promised to bless Ishmael. Remember, Ishmael was not God's idea. He was born out of Abraham and Sarah's inability to wait for a blessing. Their impatience created tremendous problems in their family and even within their marriage. That doesn't matter, however. God won't let the problems we create simply go away. No, he chooses to bless our problems and redeem them for a great purpose.

From Ishmael descended a great Arab nation. From Isaac descended a great Jewish nation. To this day, some in these nations would like the other to just go away. Yet until we learn to respect the problems God has blessed, we'll never have peace.

❦

On the Move

And immediately they left their nets and followed him.

Mark 1:18

READ MARK 1:16-20

It is amazing how much movement there is in the Bible. Abraham and Sarah had to leave everything in their hometown to chase a great dream. Later, their descendents moved from slavery to the Promised Land. It was when the Hebrews felt settled in the land that their problems started. Before long, they were in exile, finding spiritual renewal. Even Jesus was constantly on the road, where all his miracles happened. So was the Church, as it moved from Jerusalem to the ends of the earth.

It is still hard to find anyone who is in a serious drama with God who is not on the move. Sometimes it is a relationship that is in motion, constantly changing, or a job. Maybe it's just the process of getting older that is forcing the changes.

All of this presents you with a choice: Will you follow Jesus to the new place or just settle into memories of the old place? Choose carefully, because the Savior is on the move, and you'll lose sight of him if you don't keep moving as well.

The first disciples kept wondering when Jesus was finally going to settle down. Eventually, however, they began to realize that the point of following Jesus was not to get to a new place. The point of following Jesus is to follow Jesus. Along the way, we come to understand that our identity is found not in where we are but in the Savior who is leading the way.

❦

The Power of No

All things are lawful for me, but not all things are beneficial.
1 Corinthians 6:12

READ 1 CORINTHIANS 6:12-20

The freedom to make choices is near the core of our identity as human beings. It is part of what it means to be made in the image of God, and it is certainly the primary means by which we retain our human dignity.

Satan's favorite temptation is to tell you that you don't have a choice about your behavior. The reason he wants you to believe this is that he wants you to be something less than human. No matter how bad your choices may have been, never give up responsibility for them, because once you do you also give up a piece of your soul.

God can forgive and redeem your guilt, but he cannot forgive those who are not responsible. And without forgiveness none of us can have our humanity restored to what it was at Creation. So the last thing you want to do is tell God that your parents, chromosomes, boss, or ex-spouse are to blame for your actions. You might as well turn in your Human Being ID card.

One of the most important things to remember about your freedom to choose, the apostle Paul says, is that you have the capacity to say "no." It's a spiritual word because it demonstrates that you are not addicted. Just because you can do something doesn't mean you have to do it. Thus, the mark of being truly free is that you are even free to choose not to use your freedom.

❧

Choosing to Listen to God

The rabble among them had a strong craving.

Numbers 11:4

Read Numbers 11:1-15

When the Hebrews left Egypt, they brought with them some people called "the rabble" who constantly complained about the hardships of the journey, about Moses, and even about God. This rabble didn't consist of many people, but they still created enormous problems. It didn't matter how many miracles God performed; the rabble could always convince the rest of the people to focus more on their fears than on God's faithfulness. They did this by appealing to the people's cravings for certainty, permanence, and abundance—all things you have to leave behind when you journey with God.

It is striking that God didn't prevent the rabble from joining this journey. Even they had a role, which was to confront the people with a choice. They each had to decide whether to trust God or the voices that made them anxious. We don't have to trust God. We can always complain. It is even more striking that when God got fed up with the people's complaining, he didn't just punish the rabble, but everyone who chose to listen to the complaint.

There is a rabble in every nation, every church, and every soul. It confronts you with a great choice. Choose carefully, for there is something seductive in hearing, "You deserve better." Perhaps the smartest choice is to spend so much time listening to God that you have little time left for the rabble.

❦

Choosing Transformation

Do not be conformed to this world, but be transformed by the renewing of your minds.

Romans 12:2

READ ROMANS 12:1-2

The word *conformed* in this verse was written in the Greek middle voice. That means that it is something we do to ourselves. Our translators could have also said, "Do not conform yourselves to this world." Here Paul is telling us that if we want to live by the values of a greedy, mean, and frightened society we can certainly do that. We just need to realize we are choosing to do that, and to realize that our choices will make us greedy, mean, and frightened.

The word *transformed* was written in the passive voice. That means it is something that is done to us. We can't transform our own lives. We can make a few improvements here and there. We can rearrange our lives, which is all that most improvement schemes accomplish. Yet when it comes to authentic, transforming change—well, that takes God.

So does all this mean we can make our lives worse, but we can't really make them better? No, not exactly. Paul also wrote that if we want to receive God's transformation, we can renew our minds. What we believe is really quite important. Ideas, thoughts, values, and systems of belief are the ways we prepare ourselves to be changed by God. Or they are the things that prevent us from being transformed. It all depends on what we put into our minds. If we want to change, we'll have to use our minds less for things that distract us from God, and more for things that renew our faith in him.

❦

Choosing Joy

*"Why was this perfume not sold for three hundred denari
and the money given to the poor?"*

John 12:5

Read John 12:1-8

Jesus was having dinner in the home of Mary and Martha and their
brother Lazarus, whom he had recently raised from the dead. During
the meal, Mary knelt in front of Jesus, took out a pound of perfume
that had cost almost a year's wages, and poured it on his feet.
Immediately, Judas blurted out, "Jesus, who authorized this expense?
Do you know what we could have done with that kind of money?"
Now that sounds like a pretty good question. What about the needs
of the poor? What about our needs? Jesus responded to Judas by
reminding him that there will always be needs, but the priority is to
know who the Savior is.

The last time we saw Mary she was again at Jesus' feet, only then it
was in tears over the death of her brother Lazarus. Now that her Savior
had brought her hopes back from the dead, what gift could she make
to him that could possibly be too elaborate?

Now bring yourself into this dinner, and take your seat. The question is, do you find yourself sitting closer to Mary, or to Judas? When
you come to Jesus, are you closer to extravagant gratitude or to complaint? If you are unhappy with your life, no amount of additional
money, success, relationships, or health will help. You will still complain about the need for more. If you are unhappy with your life, the
only way to find joy is in giving thanks.

❦

Choosing to Love

I do not do what I want, but I do the very thing I hate.
Romans 7:15

READ ROMANS 7

Scripture consistently claims that we make our best progress on the Christian journey by recognizing how lost we have become. Why is that? Why is falling into error such an important part of the discovery of spiritual truth? Doesn't God think we can do anything for ourselves?

In the Bible we are certainly given a great deal of exhortation to live as responsible men and women. We are responsible for choosing whom we will serve, with whom we will conduct our lives, and what we will do with the few fleeting years we have. God is not trying to turn us into angels who have overcome our wills and the freedom to make decisions. To the contrary, what God is hoping, most of all, is that we will choose to love him and his kingdom as much as he loves us.

This means that Christians have to take their choices very seriously as they travel down life's road. The spiritual criteria for evaluating any choice is whether or not it has left us open to God. That is why confession is such a helpful milestone along the journey. It invites us to see that even our best choices have been tainted by self-serving insecurities. In confession we take responsibility for our bad choices, ask forgiveness, and are left humbled by our need for God. Thus confession opens up a space in our lives that was not there before, an open space for God to enter. With his presence, we are then guided away from the road that leads to nowhere, and find ourselves on the path back to God.

❦

Wholly Business or Holy Business?

"The place on which you are standing is holy ground."

Exodus 3:5

READ EXODUS 3:1-10

It started out as just another ordinary day at work. Moses was doing the same thing he had done for forty years—taking care of sheep. Yet then he saw a bush that was on fire, and he heard the voice of God telling him, "Remove your sandals, for this is holy ground." Moses had probably been past that bush a lot. Day after day, month after month, year in and year out, he walked by it while he worked. He always thought it was just a bush. Now he saw it was on holy ground. And on holy ground anything can happen.

It's fascinating that we all ask essentially the same questions about work. "Do I really enjoy what I am doing?" "How do I cope with the stress?" "How do I meet all the expectations of me?" The young parent who stays at home with children asks those questions. So does the CEO of a major corporation. Day after day we all walk around the familiar landscape of our workplace. In fact, it's so familiar that we can't see that there is holy business going on.

The question we should be asking is, "For whom do I really work?" Our culture has taught us to accept too sharp a distinction between secular and sacred ground. God gets Sundays, but at work there is a different lord and there are different expectations. Yet if you choose to work for God, all ground becomes holy, and every assignment becomes a liturgy of worship. If you pay attention, you can even see the miracles.

✿

Help With the Choices

Eli perceived that the Lord was calling the boy.

1 Samuel 3:8

READ 1 SAMUEL 3:1-18

When the Lord called young Samuel in the sanctuary, Samuel thought it was the high priest Eli who was speaking. Three times the Lord called, and three times Samuel went running to Eli saying, "Here I am, for you called me." Finally, Eli figured out what was going on. So he taught Samuel how to listen, and respond, to the call of the Lord. Samuel already had the right words, and he was certainly trying to respond. Yet he was responding to the wrong person.

We all need an Eli in our lives. His role is to teach us first how to worship and then how to respond to the call of God upon our lives. Today we may call Eli a mentor or a spiritual director. In previous years, we would have called him a discipler, teacher, or best of all, a priest. The job of priests is not to draw people to themselves, but to the calling of God. None of us can discern God's call on our own. When we try that, we just become confused, because we are more accustomed to listening to what human voices are calling us to be and do. Yet the priest can train our ears to listen to the persistent, still small voice of God.

It doesn't matter how old you are, you never outgrow your need to have a priest, or to be one for someone else. Giving someone to God is a part of every holy calling. So who is your Eli? And for whom are you Eli?

❦

Out of the Labyrinth, Into the Light

Where there is no vision, the people perish.
                                        Proverbs 29:18, KJV

READ PROVERBS 29:18

In his book, *Hope in Time of Abandonment,* Jacques Ellul has traced the tragic ironies of our age. Our society considers itself scientific and technologically sophisticated, yet we act irrationally with personal relationships. While living in the land of the free, we feel stuck in jobs we do not like but must keep to afford lifestyles that do not give us joy. Never before have a people taken such pride in their individuality and yet still complained about the mythic "they" who are to blame for their problems. Every day we confront more opportunity than any people in history, but at night we lie in bed awake, stare at the ceiling, and wonder where life is going.

These are the problems of a people who have lost their vision and have become confused about the purpose of life. In such a time it is critical that the Church be clear about its vision. Its purpose is to help us remember our purpose. In the words of the Shorter Catechism, we exist to glorify God and enjoy him forever. When we are clear about that, the rest of life becomes clearer. We start asking different questions and we make very different choices. We give up worrying about things like where life is going, and we find joy in receiving the grace of God that comes along the way. Only then can we stop trying to become something else and start glorifying God by being who we are.

❦

Providence

"Who knows? Perhaps you have come to the kingdom for such a time as this."

Esther 4:14

READ ESTHER 4:1-16

Esther was a Jew who had somehow become queen of Persia. She also managed to somehow discover a plot to assassinate the king, and thus earned his deep gratitude. Then when a movement developed to exterminate all the Jews in the land, she discovered she was somehow the only person who was in a position to stop it. Yet to do that, she had to risk losing all the wonderful things that had somehow come her way.

Most of us know that we have been blessed in life. Even if we consider ourselves to be hard workers, we know we could never have earned the life we now have. In fact, the things that we cherish the most are things that somehow have been given to us. Friends, family, children, talents, skills, opportunities, health, love—all of them are gifts.

Why do we have these gifts? In part, it is because, like any loving father, God enjoys giving these things to his children. Yet there is another reason. These gifts didn't just fall to us somehow. There is a purpose, in the providence of God, for us to have the lives we do. We may spend much of our lives not really knowing what that purpose is. Yet one day we'll each encounter an opportunity to do what only we can do for the kingdom of God.

Don't worry about missing that moment. It will be painfully clear because it will involve enormous risk. Worry instead about having the courage to do the right thing.

❦

Choosing the Curse

See I am setting before you today a blessing and a curse.
Deuteronomy 11:26

Read Deuteronomy 11:18-32

Life is filled with choices, and many of them are quite difficult. The more we value something, like our careers or relationships, the harder it is to make choices about them. That's because we are terrified of making a mistake about something so important.

From the perspective of heaven, however, most of our choices about careers and relationships don't really matter all that much. The Bible has already told us all that God cares to say about such matters. No, you can't murder your boss. Yes, you can quit your job and get another one if you want. No, you don't have to be married. Yes, you do have to forgive those who hurt you.

"Now," the Bible would tell us, "let's move on to something really important. Do you want a blessing or a curse from God?"

According to Deuteronomy, to ask for God's blessings is to ask for God. To ask for a curse is to ask for a different god, like a relationship or your career. The curse is that the true God will allow you to make these things your god, just long enough for them to suck away your soul.

I'm not sure why people keep choosing the curse, unless it's because they would rather have a god they can control than the Mysterious One they cannot. Yet only by bowing before the Mystery can we receive a mysterious future. And only then do we know the blessing of being truly alive.

❧

Learning to Love Leah

So Rachel died, and she was buried on the way to ...
Bethlehem.

Genesis 35:19

READ GENESIS 35:16-20

Rachel and Leah, Jacob's two wives, were sisters. Rachel was the wife he had always wanted. He worked seven years for her father in order to marry her, but the morning after his wedding, he discovered he had been given Leah. So Jacob had to work another seven years to get Rachel.

If you have ever been in a relationship, it isn't long before you discover that the person you love is both Rachel and Leah—the love you want and the love you've got. This is just as true for women as it is for men. You can work for a long time trying to turn Leah into Rachel, but Leah will always be Leah. And Jacob will always be Jacob. So you will never enjoy your relationships until you accept the people you have in your life for who they are. Yet you'll never be able to do that until you receive them as God's gifts. This understanding means your struggle with relationships is first of all a struggle with God.

After Jacob spent the night of his life wrestling with God, it changed everything for him. The proof of this is that when Rachel died during a journey, Jacob just buried her alongside the road, because he was finally able to walk away from the trophy wife. Yet when Leah died, he had her buried in the family plot with Abraham and Sarah, Isaac and Rebecca, right next to the place where he would rest forever. In the end, Jacob chose the gift over the fantasy.

❦

Holy Reluctance

[Moses] said, "O my Lord, please send someone else."
Exodus 4:13

READ EXODUS 4:1-17

Have you ever noticed how few of God's leaders applied for the job? Most of them had settled into perfectly satisfactory lives and were not eager to be interrupted by God's call. Moses is a good example of this reluctance. Long ago he had tried to help a Hebrew slave who was being beaten by an Egyptian taskmaster. That plan didn't turn out so well, and Moses had had to get out of town fast. Having been burnt as a do-gooder, he was hesitant to get back into the ministry.

It is also interesting that those in the Bible who did apply to be of service, like the rich young ruler, were usually turned away. Perhaps that is because the last thing the Lord needs are our plans for helping him out. At the burning bush, it was God who was coming up with the ideas, and that seemed to make all the difference.

I find that most people know what they ought to be doing for the Lord. They just aren't sure they want to pay the cost, and maybe they doubt they can really make a difference. It's easier to settle for the life we have. This sense of holy reluctance is not a bad thing, as long as we still respond to the call. It will keep us from getting confused about who the real Savior is. It is also a clear indication that it is God who is calling, and not the messianic pretender who lives in all of us.

❦

Leaving the Harvest to God

So let us not grow weary in doing what is right, for we will reap at harvest time, if we do not give up.

Galatians 6:9

READ GALATIANS 6:7-10

At the end of my first year of seminary, I was just far enough along to be really discouraged. All the other students seemed so much smarter than I. So many of them had such a dramatic sense of calling from God, while I still hadn't run across any burning bushes. We spent our weekends working in churches, and my first year was spent futilely trying to get a youth group going in a church where the average age of the members was about seventy-five. I was not a stunning success. There were two years to go before I would graduate, and I was starting to wonder if this wasn't a long walk down the wrong road. I was pretty sure that I belonged in the ministry, but I couldn't figure out why God would want me. I had so little to show him after that first year.

Then I received a letter from my mother in which she quoted this verse: "let us not grow weary in doing what is right." She reminded me that God was more interested in my faithfulness than in my success. That may have been the most important thing I learned from seminary. Usually, we do eventually see the harvest from our labors, but the Christian life is not focused on that. The harvest is really God's business, and we are only the hired hands. For us, joy is found in the daily opportunity to do what is right, just because we know it is right.

❦

On Living for Today

"I go to prepare a place for you."

John 14:3

READ JOHN 14:1-14

We have a lot of questions about heaven. We wonder which biblical images of heaven and hell are literal, and which are metaphors. When does the soul rise from the dead? Now, or on the last day? Paul wrote about the dead sleeping, but Jesus told the thief on the cross, "Today you will be with me in paradise." The Bible doesn't give us many clear details on this topic, so apparently God doesn't want us to focus on the next life but to live in this life with the hope of heaven.

People who believe in heaven act different from others. They make choices more easily, because they believe their choices are seldom ultimate. They are less cautious with life, more likely to laugh at themselves, and a lot more likely to give themselves to others. That's because they don't waste much time trying to be their own savior. What we do know about heaven is that no one gets there by being good enough. We get there only because Jesus Christ has prepared a place for us.

Heaven proclaims that the end of our stories are already written. By the grace of God, they end wonderfully. There's not a thing we can do to make them end any better. Since the ending is already written, that frees us to enjoy the mystery of today without worrying about where it is heading.

All we really know about tomorrow is that Jesus is waiting for us, in life and in death. So we might as well live as if today is all we have, which, of course, it is.

❦

Trusting in God

"We are not able to go up against this people, for they are stronger than we."

Numbers 13:31

READ NUMBERS 13:25-33

After two long years of journey through the desert, the Hebrews were finally at the southern border of the Promised Land. God told them to send twelve spies "into the land which I am giving to the Israelites." The spies discovered that the land was far more glorious than they had dreamed. Yet they also found giants living there. Ten of the spies returned from their trip to report that the Hebrews shouldn't even bother entering. When they saw the giants, they said, "We seemed to ourselves like grasshoppers."

There is always a Promised Land ahead, and there are always giants that stand in the way of our entrance. Compared to the giants, the ten spies were right. They were pretty weak and did not have what it took to defeat the giants. Of course, that was the wrong comparison. The real match was between the giants and God. Two of the spies, Joshua and Caleb, saw that and begged the people to trust God and move ahead. Yet the people were afraid, and so they wandered aimlessly in the desert until that generation died.

I am impressed that God honors our choices so much. He has prepared a hopeful future for us and promised to place it in our hands. All we have to do is to keep moving toward it. The giants that stand in the way are merely opportunities for us to exercise faith. Or they can intimidate us away from the dream. It's our choice.

❦

Answers We Already Know

"You are the light of the world."

Matthew 5:14

READ MATTHEW 5:13-16

When Horace Bushnell began his teaching career at Yale Divinity School, he struggled to increase his faith. He prayed that God would give him more light, thinking that was what he needed to become a better teacher of ministers. In time, he realized that it made little sense to ask God for more light when he had not been faithful to the insights God had already given him. In his diary he wrote, "I have moved from the agony of questions I cannot answer to the agony of answers I cannot escape."

It can be an evasion to go on asking questions when we have not given ourselves to the answers that we already know. We know that in Jesus Christ God has made many things perfectly clear. For example, he taught us that love is better than hate—even when it comes to our enemies. Jesus was never ambiguous about our need to live dependent upon the mercy of God. He consistently taught his disciples that since life was such a fragile thing, it was best to give it away to things that make an eternal difference.

What most of us need is not all of the pieces to life's puzzle, but enough courage to live by the clear insights we have. Our lives have been placed into the midst of personal relationships where we have been called to live in love and joy. We have also been placed in a dark world that is desperate for any light it can find. There really isn't that much question about what we should do. The real question is whether or not we will do it.

❦

To Lay Down Your Life

"I lay down my life in order to take it up again.... I have power to lay it down, and I have power to take it up again."
John 10:17-18

READ JOHN 10:1-21

On Palm Sunday the cheering crowds in Jerusalem thought Jesus had come to fulfill their expectations. As the story goes, things took a turn for the worse later in the week. They then realized Jesus was not who they thought he was, and so they nailed him onto a cross. Yet Jesus made it clear long before he arrived in Jerusalem that the only reason he was going to end up on a cross was because he had chosen to do that. That means Jesus was a Savior, not a victim.

As you follow Jesus, you will find that he often invites you to carry a cross as well. Maybe you will bear a cross as a parent, or in the office, or in the time you give to others. Yet no one can make you do that. You have to choose the cross, or you will simply be a victim who is manipulated by the relentless expectations of others.

As long as you choose to serve, you will keep power. You can continue to bear this cross, or you can stop. It's your choice. You have the power to lay down your life, and you have the power to take it up again. Never, ever, give up the power to stop serving, because you'll never be able to give anything resembling the salvation of Christ unless your service comes as a gracious gift.

❦

Inheriting Tradition

Keep these words that I am commanding you today in your heart. Recite them to your children and talk about them when you are at home.

Deuteronomy 6:6-7

READ DEUTERONOMY 6:4-9

These days it is complicated to figure out how children inherit values. Most of us cannot spend the time with kids that parents did in earlier years. While we are away at work, the kids are attending schools that strive to be "value neutral."

Some today even reject the whole concept of inheriting values. It seems too arbitrary. No longer raising children to participate in the traditions of ancestors, we now more more commonly raise kids "to make good choices." Certainly children need to know how to make choices, but they also need a moral framework for those choices. To just give children a choice on whether or not to be religious doesn't really offer them freedom. More often, it only conveys the parents' ambivalence about their own faith.

Each generation questions the values they receive from their parents. Typically, they eventually embrace or reshape those values. Yet that assumes parents have given their children the gift of knowing a moral value when they see one. Now, we are discovering that many young adults have nothing worth rebelling against. They are as "value neutral" as the sterile systems in which they are raised.

Values, certainly spiritual values, are not à la carte options that can be either picked up or discarded. Rather, they are a way of life that can be modeled only by parents who believe in them. In the family of God, we still have some ancestral truths. If we live as if they are true, they will be true for our kids as well.

❦

Choosing Silence

If any think they are religious, and do not bridle their tongues ... their religion is worthless.

James 1:26

READ JAMES 1:19-27

When we were children we used to say to each other, "Sticks and stones may break my bones, but words will never hurt me." Remember that? Well, we were wrong. Very wrong. As adults we now know that some of the worst hurts in our lives have come from angry words.

There are some words that you must never say, even if you feel like it. That's because they can't be taken back and will only continue to hurt. For example, no one ever forgets hearing, "I don't love you." You can try reassurances that you didn't really mean it. You can apologize a hundred times. Yet the awful words will just keep ripping holes in the heart of the person who heard them.

When James wrote to the churches, he was very concerned by how much hurt people were causing through the careless use of words. Basically, James' message is to stop talking so much. Stop talking about each other. Stop talking about your complaints. Stop talking about your great accomplishments. Just stop it. It doesn't only hurt others, it also hurts you by distorting the image of Jesus Christ in your life.

The only time Jesus would ever talk about someone else was in prayer, when he would say things like, "Father, forgive them." So if whatever you are about to say can't be turned into a prayer, then you may just want to pray about having something better to say.

FIVE

Into the Hands of the Living God

❦

No Fear

Do not fret—it leads only to evil.

Psalm 37:8

READ PSALM 37:1-9

Have you ever made a good decision when you were frightened? Probably not. Yet the chances are good that fear has caused some of the worst choices you've made.

Most of us are pretty good at discerning the "worst-case scenario." Once this imagined disaster enters our minds, it takes over our lives. We fret constantly. We keep trying to think of ways to avoid the disaster. We may even pray, "Please God, don't let that happen."

That is certainly a good prayer. Yet once you have placed something in God's hands, it is best to leave it there. After all, God has really good hands. They once created light and beauty out of darkness and chaos. In Jesus Christ, God's hands healed the sick, fed the hungry, cast out evil, and even raised the dead. So do you really want to try to wrestle control over the future out of God's hands and give it to the thing that makes you afraid? That is what fretting does. It is a choice, a foolish choice, to live as if God is not God.

People who maintain faith in God during frightening times do not believe they will always succeed. Yet they are never afraid to fail. That is because, as Jesus told us, nothing can ever pull us out of the Father's hands. Once we are clear about that, life becomes less of a worry to be controlled and more of a mystery to be savored.

ł

Taking Great Risks

"On finding one pearl of great value, he went and sold all that he had and bought it."

Matthew 13:46

Read Matthew 13:44-50

When we were children, our parents repeatedly told us, "Be careful." Apparently they said the words enough to make them stick. We still hear the phrase every day, only now it comes from the back of our minds. "Be careful." Maybe we overlearned the lesson. When it comes to things like health and morality, being careful is important. Yet there are other times when it is not so wise. Like when you are trying to get into the kingdom of heaven.

Jesus once said the kingdom of heaven is like a man who sells everything to buy a single pearl. Clearly, this is not being careful. What could make him so reckless? He would have to be certain that this one thing was more valuable than everything else. That's the way you have to come to God. In fact, it would actually be reckless to approach God carefully. You had better come with sheer abandon and place all of life into his hands.

People who have given everything to God are then free to live with more passion, because they are not worried about losing things. They already did that when they came to God. Nor are they as worried about making mistakes, which frees them to take adventurous risks. The last thing you want to do is show up at the gates of heaven, saying, "I don't need grace. I made no mistakes, because I never risked using my life." That will not play well in heaven.

❦

An Instrument of God

His disciples took him by night and let him down through an opening in the wall, lowering him in a basket.

Acts 9:25

READ ACTS 9:23-30

This is how Paul's first evangelistic campaign ended. It was not a stunning success. It all began when Paul was charging up to Damascus to persecute the church. Along the way, however, he was converted by a vision of Jesus. After spending less than a week in town being taught by the other disciples of Christ, Paul immediately began to preach in the synagogues. It wasn't long before the people who had hired him to persecute the church were now plotting to kill him. So late at night he had to sneak out of town in a basket.

As he was being lowered down the wall, Paul had to be confused. This was the end of the strangest week in his life. His life was out of control. Or rather, it was not in his control.

This humble escape is actually a wonderful sign that Paul really had encountered the grace of Jesus Christ. When he was a persecutor, we are told that Paul "ravaged the church." He dragged the followers of Christ away in chains, because he was determined to get a job done. When we are committed only to our goals, we ravage others, who get hurt along the way. After converting Paul, the Lord called him his "instrument." The difference between being a ravager and being an instrument is that the instrument exists simply to be used in the hands of someone else. The Lord can pick up his instruments, put them down, or save them to be used somewhere else.

❦

Effective Leadership

"Can we find anyone else like this?—one in whom is the spirit of God?"

Genesis 41:38

READ GENESIS 41:25-46

This is what Pharaoh said after meeting Joseph. Clearly he was impressed, because he made Joseph second only to himself in ruling over Egypt. It's important to remember that at the time Joseph was a convict in jail. Prior to that, he was a slave, and prior to that he was a foreigner. So it wasn't Joseph's résumé that impressed Pharaoh. There must have been plenty of people with impeccable résumés hanging around the Egyptian court. No, the thing that impressed Pharaoh was the Spirit of God that he saw in this lowly man, Joseph.

To be filled with the Holy Spirit is to have so much of God within you that others see neither your failures nor your successes, but your God. The Spirit doesn't erase your personality, but restores you to being the person you were created to be from the beginning—one who reflects God's glory. Thus, the more Spirit there is within you, the more you show the real you, and the less you are defined by either heartaches or achievements. Your God-given character shines through all of that, which is what makes you so very distinctive.

Our society is searching today for new role models in all areas of life. We've seen a lot of people with impressive credentials, but that is really beside the point. What we want to see is someone whose spirit reminds us of what we were all created to be. That's pretty rare. And that is why we call it leadership.

❦

Surrender to Christ

We take every thought captive to obey Christ.

2 Corinthians 10:5

READ 2 CORINTHIANS 10:1-6

Paul had a very dramatic relationship with the church at Corinth. It is obvious he loved this congregation, but no other church drove him crazy like this one. They were divisive, argumentative, arrogant, and constantly challenging his authority. So why didn't he just abandon them and spend his time taking care of the churches that were easier to love? My guess is that Paul recognized himself in this congregation. Their problems were the same as his. Thus, his counsel to the church comes with great authority, born out of God's work in his own life.

Paul had told the Corinthians, "We do not wage war according to human standards." The problem was not that the members of the church had disagreements. Everybody faces disagreements. The problem was that they settled them by human standards. According to human standards we draw lines in the sand, spin the facts our way, insist on what we want, and allow our hearts to be taken captive to hurt and anger.

There is another way, Paul claims. It begins by making every thought captive to Christ. This means that the real battleground is found in your own life. Before you say a word, or hear a word, you must first surrender it to Jesus Christ, who alone can save you. That makes the battle his to wage. You have already surrendered, not to your opponent but to Christ. Don't be surprised if the Savior walks away from battles you think are important. Sometimes salvation comes from the discovery that you were worried about the wrong issue.

❦

Holding Hands

I held out my hands all day long to a rebellious people, who walk in a way that is not good.

Isaiah 65:2

Read Isaiah 65:1-7

Some folks always seem to be a few steps behind God—like Moses, for example. At the burning bush, God told him to deliver the Hebrews from Pharaoh, but Moses had settled into his life as shepherd and was not eager to leave. We stay far behind God when we get too committed to a comfortable place in life. This is not a place where we belong, and it is not even a place that is good for us. It is just comfortable. My experience has been that God leads us away from comfortable places, because only then do we recognize our need for a savior.

Other folks are always a few steps ahead of God, and David would be a good example of that. He constantly came up with great plans, building programs, and political strategies that were news to God. People like David find it irresistible to develop these improvement programs because God seems to move so slowly. They feel that they had better help him out with these good ideas they have. Yet typically, it is when we run ahead of God that we get really lost. Again, the good news here is that if we realize we are lost, we are ready for a savior.

The common dynamic for all who walk with God seems to be recognizing our need for a savior. He's not an easy companion in life. As God, he will always take the lead—not to lose us or frustrate us, but simply to make sure that we are holding his hand tightly. Yet in order to hold God's hands, we'll have to let go of things like comfort and great plans.

❦

On the Heels of Fear

Living in the fear of the Lord and in the comfort of the Holy Spirit ...

Acts 9:31

READ ACTS 9

At first, these appear to be contradictory emotions. How can we be comforted by the Spirit of a God we fear? Ironically, we cannot be comforted by God unless we fear him. And if we knew the level of comfort that God would bring into our lives we would fear him even more.

We fear God not because he is the angry judge, but because he is beyond our control. In fact, it is he who controls our lives. He takes us to places we had not planned to go and to a future we had never imagined; he gives us gifts we do not want and burdens we never knew we could bear. And along the way, God molds and shapes our lives. If we pay attention to this good creation emerging within us, we will find comfort on the heels of our fear.

We have long thought that comfort is found by overcoming all reasons to be afraid. Yet the Holy Spirit teaches just the opposite. Comfort is found by the terrifying discovery that we are in the hands of the God who once rolled back the dark chaos of earth to create beauty and light. As we watch this new creation in the making, it may seem still chaotic. However, that is only because God has not yet completed what he has begun. You can never judge a work of art until it is finished, and this work won't be finished until the Spirit has completely transformed your life into the image of Jesus.

❦

God's Changes in Our Lives

"If this plan or this undertaking is of human origin it will fail; but if it is of God, you will not be able to overthrow them."
Acts 5:38-39

READ ACTS 5:27-42

After Peter and some of the apostles were imprisoned, they were given the opportunity to tell their Jewish leaders the story of Jesus' life, death, and resurrection. It made some of these leaders so angry that they wanted to kill the apostles. Yet a wise old Pharisee named Gamaliel reminded everyone of the failed messianic ventures of two men named Theudas and Judas the Galilean. Both of them had had a following, but the movement had died soon after the leader was killed. All human movements eventually fail. Yet if the Jesus movement had been started by God, Gamaliel reasoned, then its success would eventually be clear. Of course, that is exactly what happened.

Sometimes we are in a quandary about the changes we are confronting. It is easy to condemn change just because we are comfortable with how things are. Of course, if we knew God was behind the change it would be easier to accept. So how do we know? One way is simply to wait and see what happens. If the new idea is of human origin, it will always fail, as all human inventions eventually do. Yet if God's hand is in this new thing, then nothing in heaven or on earth can overthrow it.

When we are confronting changes, it makes all the difference in the world to believe that God is sovereign. We are not asked to be certain of every change that blows like the wind through our lives. We are asked only to be certain of God.

❦

Giving Ourselves Back to the Savior

For it is God who is at work in you, enabling you both to will and to work for his good pleasure.

Philippians 2:13

READ PHILIPPIANS 2:12-18

St. Hilary of Tours cautioned that we must always avoid the blasphemous anxiety of doing God's work for him. In other words, we are all invited to work in God's kingdom, but only God can really do that which he has in mind. The Lord expressed this through the prophet Isaiah when he said, "You are my witnesses." It's the job of a witness to watch for God's salvation, but not to make it happen. Only those who are convinced they have a Savior can avoid the temptation of becoming one themselves.

This means that much of the time we wonder where our lives are heading. Some of us plod along with faithfulness, day after day, but we cannot see the glorious creation that God has promised. Others of us are petrified at the turns life has taken. Sometimes we grow so anxious over the confusion that we decide to take over and complete things according to our own ideas of what God should be doing. That's usually when the big disasters start. As Christians, we must develop a regular habit of giving ourselves, our families and jobs, and certainly our Church back to the Savior. We can do that only if we hold our expectations about the future pretty loosely.

God has a way of always getting what he wants. He is at work even if we can't see it, and even if the stuff we do see looks anything but divine. Yet if we are faithful, in time, usually with hindsight, we discover God's plans are much more thrilling than the smaller ideas we had in mind.

☙

The Marvelous Gift

"He has been raised from the dead, and indeed he is going ahead of you to Galilee; there you will see him."

Matthew 28:7

READ MATTHEW 28:1-10

The real question of Easter is not whether we believe in the resurrection, but whether we have encountered the risen Jesus. Most people can easily live with a vague belief that Jesus really did rise from the dead. Yet if it makes no impact on their lives then one wonders about the power of this belief. It was not enough for the first disciples to simply hear that Jesus had risen. They had to see him for themselves. According to Matthew, the place where they were told to look for him was back home in Galilee. Home is where we assume life will be predictable. Yet since that first Easter nothing is predictable. If you don't look at the familiar routines of your life tomorrow a little differently, then you have missed the best part of the Easter story. As the angel said, Jesus has gone ahead. He is waiting with the marvelous gift of mystery.

"So the women left with fear and great joy" (Mt 28:8). Our joy and our fear live pretty close to each other. If you do not feel joy, it is probably because you think the story will end with the loss of your job, your relationships, or your health. We try to squeeze all the life out of these things while we still have them, but there is no joy in that. Joy follows the terrifying realization that we don't know how the story of our lives will end. That is because God is still writing it.

Leave Your Failures in His Hands

Shake off the dust from your feet as you leave.

Matthew 10:14

READ MATTHEW 10:5-15

At this time, Jesus had just given his disciples a mission to travel throughout Israel, preaching, healing, and casting out demons. Then he cautioned them about the resistance they would meet from those who preferred to keep living as if there were no God. It is interesting that Jesus didn't tell the disciples to argue with those who disagreed with them. He didn't tell them to try to convince, prove, or debate. Instead, Jesus told his disciples to shake the dust off their feet and keep moving.

We can't try to do something as important as offering grace, healing, or freedom from evil without meeting resistance. When we spend too much time in unproductive debates about these things, it may have more to do with our need to be victorious than with our desire to see God victorious. God can take care of his own arguments. Our mission is just to witness, or to watch, what he is doing in people's lives.

We know that we have to give God our moments of great success, but that isn't very hard. When someone compliments us, we can easily say something like, "God gave me the power." It is much harder to also give him our defeats, and leave the failure in his hands. Yet if we don't do that, the dust will stick not only to our feet but also to our hearts. Eventually we will stop trying to reach out to others, and our hearts will be left dusty and unused. Then it is God who will be arguing with us.

❦

Invested in God

Where your treasure is, there your heart will be also.

Matthew 6:21

READ MATTHEW 6:19-21

Often when the Bible introduces a new character to us, the person is holding something he or she treasures. It's something on which this person is betting his or her life. Abraham was clinging to what little family he had. Moses was holding onto a shepherd's staff. David had a slingshot. Some of the disciples were holding fishing nets when we first met them. The rich, young ruler was clutching his wealth tightly. A poor widow was holding two copper coins, all that she had.

It may be money, a weapon, a profession, or a relationship. It may be little or a lot. Yet before these people encountered God, they always had some cherished treasure. And they held it so tightly, because with this treasure life seemed secure and hopeful. Without it, they felt vulnerable in the harsh world. So it's not surprising that God always asked these people if they would give him this treasure. It was the only way he could be their God.

This is why Jesus said, "Where your treasure is, there will your heart be also." When Jesus made this statement, he was talking about earthly treasures like money, which, as he said, nobody gets to keep after they die. The only things that we can carry with us across the river of death are eternal treasures like faith, hope, and love. If you want to know if you have invested your heart in these things, you need to take a hard look at your checkbook, because your treasure and your heart will always be in the same place.

❦

Dreaming a Greater Dream

So when Joseph came to his brothers ... they took him and threw him into a pit.

Genesis 37:23-24

READ GENESIS 37:1-24

A little too "special" for his own good, Joseph wasn't easy to be around. He was clearly Daddy's favorite, and he was always overdressed. Yet the worst thing about Joseph was that he kept talking about his great dreams. If your little brother shared dreams like these with you, well, you would throw him in a pit as well.

In one of his dreams the sun, the moon, and eleven stars all bowed before Joseph. His eleven brothers caught the metaphor and weren't impressed. Even his father thought that dream might have gone a bit over the top. If Joseph could have just settled into the routines of the family farm like his brothers, he could have had a safe, uneventful life. Yet his dreams were the cause of all of his problems. They were also his salvation.

The world has always been hard on dreamers. It was hard on Joseph, Paul, Martin Luther, and Martin Luther King Jr., and even on Jesus. If you live with a great dream, you'll never settle for being one of the masses who don't rock the boat. You'll never settle for just tending your own garden, or for staying out of the way, and you'll never be able to stop talking about your dream. Yet don't be surprised if people try to shut you up. It doesn't matter whether your dream came from God. Others will still try to put you back in the pit. That's because your dream is a judgment upon those who've settled for playing it safe.

❦

Your New Name

You shall be called by a new name that the mouth of the Lord will give.

Isaiah 62:2

READ ISAIAH 62:1-5

The Bible depicts several instances where God changed someone's name. Abram and Sarai became Abraham and Sarah, the father and mother of many nations. Jacob's name was eventually changed to Israel, meaning one who struggles with God. When Jesus met Cephas, he called him Peter, the rock of the church. Saul, the persecutor, underwent a great conversion and became Paul the Apostle.

Sometimes, the new name was given early on in the person's journey with God, as if it were a new identity inviting them into a new future. At other times it came near the end of their lives, as if it were a summary statement of their drama with God. In either case the new name always described God's creativity in their lives.

It makes me wonder if maybe God has a new name for all of us that would tell our story and capture the essence of his work in us. My hunch is that this new name would be pretty different from the identity we wear publicly. Maybe it would be something like, "finally learned to receive life," or possibly, "discovered God was faithful after all."

The chances are great that we may spend our lives without ever knowing that new name, and even greater that if we did know the name we would want to keep it a secret. Yet I would bet that if you heard the name called, you would probably turn your head. In fact, if you were called by your real name, you would probably drop everything and follow the one who called.

❧

The Cost of Salvation

"My eyes have seen your salvation."

Luke 2:30

READ LUKE 2:22-38

It was Jewish custom to bring the firstborn male child to the temple to dedicate him to the Lord and offer a sacrifice. It happened every day. When Joseph and Mary brought their new son Jesus to the temple, they were just one more ordinary couple, doing a very ordinary thing. Yet a man named Simeon took their little baby in his arms and praised God, saying, "Now I can die in peace, for my eyes have seen your salvation."

All new parents think their babies are special. Yet most still have very ordinary dreams for them. They just want their children to be healthy and happy. Simeon cautioned Mary, saying, "It will hurt you to see what our salvation costs this child. It will feel like a sword piercing your soul." From the beginning, Jesus was identified as our Savior. All of Mary's precious, ordinary dreams would be sacrificed as he grew older.

What's changed since Christ came into the world? That all depends on what you are carrying through life with you. If, like Mary, you are holding your salvation, nothing will be ordinary for you again.

You can't keep holding Jesus without eventually letting go of your ordinary dreams. There will be times when that will feel like a sword in your soul. Yet it is still your salvation.

❦

Keep Moving

"Those who want to save their life will lose it, and those who lose their life for my sake will find it."

Matthew 16:25

READ MATTHEW 16:24-28

It is amazing how much of the Bible portrays Jesus' invitation to lose our lives. The disciples had to leave behind fishing nets, family members, and all sources of security if they were to follow. Why does faith in Jesus demand such abandonment?

Maybe it's because the greatest danger to life is to try to secure it. We want a sense of meaning and joyful purpose to our lives. We want it so much that every time we get close to it we try to nail it down. Yet Jesus calls his disciples to keep moving. Nowhere is this more obvious than with our expectations.

Any relationship demands that we leave behind the expectations we had when we began our lives together. Your spouse of fifty years will not be the same person you married. The children you intended to raise will rarely be the children you receive. In time, you'll even discover that Jesus is different from the person you expected him to be. You have to keep moving.

Not only do we have to leave behind expectations of the future; we also have to leave behind the hurts of the past and the present. This is hardest of all, because over time we have made friends with our hurt. I am always amazed by this, but I have discovered that people prefer the misery they know to the mystery they do not.

❦

Don't Count on the Past

The Lord said to me, "Enough from you! Never speak to me of this matter again!"

Deuteronomy 3:26

READ DEUTERONOMY 3:23-29

Moses never got over the fact that God would not let him lead the Hebrews all the way into the Promised Land. Over the last forty years of the wilderness journey God had been so merciful to a contentious, difficult people whose love of God was seasonal at best. Yet Moses had been an exemplar of devotion to God, except for one unfortunate moment near the end. The people had complained about the lack of water again, and God had told Moses to ask a rock to deliver up the water. Yet Moses was so angry at the people that he struck the rock with his powerful staff. It doesn't seem like that great an excess. In fact, years earlier God had even told him to strike a different rock for water. Yet this time, Moses was supposed to command the rock to give water.

The problem, it seems, was Moses' dependence on that staff. It had once performed miracles before Pharaoh, and had parted the Red Sea, and had done many other magnificent things over the years. Now, however, God expected Moses to do something new. There were great challenges ahead in the Promised Land, and the people would need a leader who was not tied to the miracles of the past. As Moses discovered, about this there was no changing God's mind.

Throughout the Bible, God is demanding of his leaders. It is a high privilege to stand between God and the people, but with privilege comes a great responsibility. Most of all, the leader's responsibility is to listen to God.

❦

The Goodness of the Garden

The serpent said ... "When you eat [of the fruit] your eyes will be opened, and you will be like God."

Genesis 3:4-5

READ GENESIS 3:1-8

A great deal of our energy is devoted to "becoming." Some of us are striving to become successful. Others are focused on becoming secure, or free, or skinny, or ... the list goes on and on. Typically, these longings all have in common the wish that we were different. We are sure that if only we could make this one adjustment to life, then we would be just fine. Sometimes we even drag God into these agendas and become preoccupied with asking ourselves, "What does he want me to become?"

It is a particularly American fantasy to think that we will be happy if we just make a few changes. So we spend way too many of our limited years trying to get to the right place. Tragically, that place only gets farther away. In the meantime life is lost as we wander away from the really good places in which God has placed us.

In our society we must remind ourselves over and over that God alone is the Creator of life. Typically we cannot see the goodness of the garden in which we live because we are blinded by the desire to be our own creator. The real challenge for Christians is not to become, but to be—to be the unique creations of God. That means we should spend less time reaching for the fruit we cannot have, and more time enjoying all the mystery and wonderful gifts of the garden we have been given.

❦

Bowing Low Enough

At the name of Jesus every knee should bend, in heaven and on earth and under the earth.

Philippians 2:10

READ PHILIPPIANS 2:1-11

Christian leaders are not invited into service because they are so talented that God has to have their help. Neither are they necessarily attracted by the responsibilities. Like the first disciples, they eventually become leaders only because they first fell in love with Jesus of Nazareth. They love him so much that they are willing to follow Jesus wherever he leads. In time they make the frightening discovery that Jesus has led them into overwhelming challenges where they are beyond their means to be of help.

It is then that Christian leaders realize that their power resides neither in their talents and abilities nor in the esteem of their office, and certainly not in their popularity with the people. As they get near the cross, they come to see that if there is any power to be found, it can come only from a Savior.

The eminent psychotherapist Carl Jung was fond of telling the story of the rabbi who was asked one day, "Why did God show himself to people so often in ancient times, but today, no one ever sees him?" The rabbi responded, "Because now no one can bow low enough to see God."

The Christian believes that the most powerful demonstration of God happened on the cross. Before leaders can see God, much less show him to others, they will have to bow down—at least as far as their knees. It is then that they will discover a vision of how God saves his people.

❦

Never Full Enough

"I will pull down my barns and build larger ones, and there I will store all my grain and my goods."

Luke 12:18

READ LUKE 12:16-21

One day a man asked Jesus to help him get more of the family inheritance. Yet Jesus refused to get involved, claiming it was impossible to win an argument about collecting wealth. You lose even if you win. To illustrate this, Jesus told him a parable about a man who had been blessed by God with abundant crops. Not knowing what to do with all his success, he decided just to build new barns to store it all. Then the man said to himself, "Soul, you have ample goods stored up for many years." Yet God said, "You fool, this very night your life is being demanded of you. And the things you have prepared, whose will they be?" (Lk 12:22).

Barn building is a quantitative approach to life that measures how successful we are by how much we have collected. We may collect different things of value. Some value money, others care more about relationships, while still others try to store up the various trophies of achievement. Yet since your barn can never be full enough of the things you care about, you will never be a success by these standards. Jesus warns us about the danger of this. "One's life does not consist in the abundance of possessions" (Lk 12:15). We don't really own anything. All of it is owned by God, who has invested these things in us. This means that success is measured not in what we collect, but in what we give back to God.

❦

Grateful for the Work of God

Let each of you lead the life that the Lord has assigned.
1 Corinthians 7:17

READ 1 CORINTHIANS 7:17-24

Children are used to hearing someone ask, "What do you want to be when you grow up?" Nobody expects a kid to say "happy." We're expecting to hear something like doctor, lawyer, homemaker, and the like. It's not uncommon for people still to be asking this same question in the middle of life, or even close to the end. Then they are asking themselves, "What do I want to be now?" The dangerous assumption behind this question is thinking that it's up to us to construct our own lives.

Those of us who hang around churches learn a different form of this question. We ask, "What is God calling me to be?" Again, nobody comes up with "happy." We, too, answer the question by focusing on work and things to do. Yet I have my doubts that God is really as concerned as we are about our jobs. It may be an American preoccupation to limit God's calling in our lives to a job description. God is a lot more concerned about the character issue.

Happiness is found not in what you do, but in learning to be grateful for what God is doing. You don't really get a life; you only receive one. The happy people are the ones who've taken the time to enjoy the gifts along the way. Their character is then one of praise to God, from whom all blessings flow.

❦

Staying Open to God's Word

The word of the Lord was rare in those days; visions were not widespread.

1 Samuel 3:1

READ 1 SAMUEL 2:22-36; 3:1

Eli was the high priest of Israel at a hard time in the life of Israel. It was also a hard time in his own life. His grown sons, who were supposed to inherit his sacred vocation, had contempt for God. They stole from the offerings that people brought to worship, and they brought their loose living right into the doors of God's sanctuary. The thing that bothered God the most about all of this was that Eli turned a blind eye to their sins. In fact, as he grew older, Eli's eyesight literally began to fail. There was a lot in the land, and in his own house, that he couldn't see. Maybe he didn't want to see it all. Maybe it just hurt too much.

It is hard for me to be too judgmental of the old priest. What parent's heart doesn't break when his children turn away from God? What religious leader's heart doesn't break when the people become mean and self-serving? After a while, it is just too hard to keep watching.

Sometimes we would like simply to remain in the house of God and not look at the problems in our homes, or hear the cries of the world around us. The problem with that strategy is that if we close our eyes and stop our ears, it will also be impossible for us to see visions and to hear the Word of the Lord. We can't be open to God without also being open to the things that break his heart.

❦

Just a Few Compromises

Then Jesus was led up by the Spirit into the wilderness to be tempted by the devil.

Matthew 4:1

READ MATTHEW 4:1-11

Sometimes people think they wouldn't be tempted if they were more spiritual. There is a highly theological term for this belief. We call it "baloney." Even Jesus was really tempted. When the devil asked him to turn a stone into bread, he knew Jesus was hungry. When the devil told him to jump from the top of the temple and be caught by angels, he was asking Jesus to be sure the Father loved him that much. When the devil offered to give Jesus all the kingdoms of the world, he appealed to Jesus' great desire to save the world. None of these temptations was about goals. No, the temptation was to seek help from the devil in reaching the goal.

I am continually impressed by the wonderful goals people have for their lives. Some want to serve their country. Others are committed to becoming a great parent in the home, a healer in the hospital, a master teacher in the school, a success in the marketplace.

So, do you think the devil is ever going to tempt you to run numbers for the mob? No, he won't ask you to give up your lofty dream and great ambitions. What the devil asks is that you simply be realistic about what it is going to take. He tells you that you just have to make a few compromises with things like values. A time will come when that will appear tempting, but you must remember that it is still a deal with the devil.

❦

Called to Joy

Like good stewards of the manifold grace of God, serve one another with whatever gift each of you has received.

1 Peter 4:10

READ 1 PETER 4:7-11

In the course of a single day we hear many voices calling to us. Most of these voices are asking for something. Our employers are asking for more work. Our kids are asking for a ride. The commercials are constantly asking us to try their product.

So when we come to church and hear the minister speak about the call of God, we may find ourselves wondering, "So what does God want from me?" It is easy for God to be just one more voice competing for our attention, our money, and our precious time.

It is important for us to remind ourselves that God doesn't need a thing from us. After all, he is God. No, the call of God is not just one more request for help. The call of God is a loving message from our Creator that reminds us why we are on this planet. It is the most significant call we will ever hear. Yet in the confusion of voices that demand our attention, it is sometimes hard to recognize God's call.

That is why we have the Bible. Ninety percent of our questions about what God wants us to do have already been answered in Scripture. The other 10 percent come by taking seriously the gifts God has given us to do his work in the world—especially the ones that give us great joy. In the words of Frederick Buechner, "The place God calls you to is the place where your deep gladness and the world's deep hunger meet."

SIX

Confessed and Forgiven

❦

The Altar of Shame

As many as the streets of Jerusalem are the altars you have set up to shame.

Jeremiah 11:13

READ JEREMIAH 11:1-14

Making sense of Jerusalem's destruction was the difficult responsibility of Jeremiah. He said it was a judgment the people brought on themselves when they turned away from the Lord and worshiped false gods.

One way you can tell that you are worshiping a false god is that it always leads to your destruction. In the past, many have sacrificed their lives on the altars of money, sex, and power. Today, there seems to be a revived interest in the altar of shame.

Shame used to be a bad thing that came with overwhelming remorse and guilt. These days, we revel in our shame. Or maybe wallowing in it. Television interviews, books, and magazines are filled with sordid descriptions of what the Bible still calls sin. People are making money off actions their grandmothers would have been too ashamed to talk about. This isn't limited to celebrity sinners. Many of us have started speaking, maybe too immodestly, about the ways we have hurt others and ourselves. It won't help to push all this back in the closet and just pretend we are righteous. Yet we do need to remember that sin is a bad thing.

I'm no fire and brimstone preacher, but even I know that when a society is no longer ashamed to be ashamed, it's on the path to self-destruction. That's because without shame, we won't seek God's forgiveness. And without forgiveness, we won't be free to stop hurting ourselves.

✻

Where We Belong

"But when he came to himself he said, 'How many of my father's hired hands have bread enough and to spare, but here I am dying of hunger! I will get up and go to my father.'"

Luke 15:17-18

READ LUKE 15:11-32

I am intrigued that the Prodigal Son first "came to himself" before he came home to the father.

Most of us spend our lives longing for home. This is not the home in which we now live, nor is it the home where we were raised. If those are good places, they serve as symbols of the spiritual home for which we are searching. Home is the place where we know we belong. It is the only place where we are fully known and fully loved, and in that grace we are at long last free to be ourselves. It has nothing to do with geography, and everything to do with returning to the Father.

We all started out in this home, but tragically we have wandered away in search of a home of our own where we can be the only authority. It isn't until we get tired of being lost and hungry that the memory of the Father's home returns to us. That is the critical moment when our lives turn around and head home again. It begins when we come to ourselves and tell the truth about who and whose we are. For we are never more ourselves than when we are with Abba Father.

❦

An Expression of Gratitude

To the pure all things are pure, but to the corrupt and unbelieving nothing is pure.

Titus 1:15

READ TITUS 1:15-16

Have you ever noticed that life is never good enough for some people, while others seem to have great joy even though their lives are plagued by problems? Some can always find reasons to give thanks. Why is that?

According to the apostle Paul the problem for those who are never happy is that "their very minds and consciences are corrupted" (Ti 1:15). It is as if a bad computer virus has corrupted all their spiritual files, making them act like something less than they are. We were all created to enjoy this brief life by finding the marks of the Creator in everything he has made. Yet sin has distorted our vision, making it hard for us to see God's good work. So instead we see only a world that is not good enough, a family that is imperfect, or friends and colleagues who don't appreciate us.

It is tempting to deal with these imperfections by trying to improve on them. We get new friends, change jobs, and bombard our family members with criticism. Yet the problem does not lie out there. The problem lies in our own corrupted minds and guilt-ridden consciences. Until we deal with these corrupted spiritual files through confession, the invitation to joy just won't compute for us. That is because joy is essentially an expression of gratitude, and nothing makes us as grateful as believing we are forgiven. When we are overwhelmed by the grace we have received, it will be hard for us to be judgmental of the world around us.

✤

The Hospital for Sinners

All have sinned and fall short of the glory of God.
Romans 3:23

READ ROMANS 3:21-26

Almost everyone has a gospel. It is what we believe in. It is what tells our story. The gospel story of the Church begins with our common need for a Savior. From the beginning we have been clear that our only Word of hope for this Savior is Jesus Christ. When we get lost or confused, we can always return to that part of our story.

My Christian tradition, the Reformed tradition, has never been too impressed by any model of the Church that reduces it to a school for saints. Churches that assume their primary role is to train the saints become preoccupied with debating. They debate each other over money, leadership, and perspectives on the truth. They debate what the church's position should be on the issues that tear at the world. Yet it is all pretty academic. When the debate is done, they will have winners and losers, but still no Savior.

My tradition has always preferred to think of the Church as a hospital for sinners where we all come to be healed by the only Savior we have. Thus, instead of debate, we believe confession is the best way to navigate through problems. Instead of educating saints, we are committed to nurturing sinners back to health.

Theology matters a great deal, but when we study theology, what we learn is that we are all more broken than we realized. That discovery will always thrust us back to our one Savior, which is the purpose of all that the Church does.

❧

A Space for God to Enter

If we confess our sins, he who is faithful and just will forgive us our sins and cleanse us from all unrighteousness.

1 John 1:9

READ 1 JOHN 1:5-10

Scripture consistently claims that we make our best progress on the Christian journey by recognizing how lost we have become. Why is that? Why is grace such a central doctrine of the faith?

Doesn't God think we can do anything for ourselves? Absolutely. In the Bible we are given a great number of exhortations to live as responsible men and women. We are responsible for choosing whom we will serve, with whom we will conduct our lives, and what we will do with the few fleeting years we have.

God is not trying to turn us into angels who have no wills or freedom to make decisions.

To the contrary, Christians have to take their choices very seriously. Yet the spiritual criteria for evaluating any choice is whether or not it has left us open to God. Nothing opens us to God quite like discovering how much we need his mercy.

In confession we take responsibility for the bad choices that have led us in the wrong direction, we ask forgiveness, and we are left humbled by our need for God. Thus confession opens up a space in our lives that was not there before. That then becomes a space for God to enter. With his presence, we are guided away from the road that leads to nowhere, and find ourselves on the path back to God.

❦

Slavery to Sin

"You will know the truth, and the truth will make you free."
John 8:32

READ JOHN 8:31-38

That phrase has been carved over the doors of a great many of our universities. That is because the founders of these schools assumed education could free humanity to create a better society. Today many of our students assume it means a college degree is the ticket to the life of their dreams. It is important to remember that Jesus, the author of the statement, had neither of these ideas in mind when he said it.

The words were said in the middle of a difficult conversation in which Jesus was explaining that only his death could free people from their slavery. Those around him protested that they were already free and slaves to nothing. We would make the same protest. We may make bad choices at times, but at least they are our choices, which we are free to make. We believe that because we want to, however, not because it is the truth. In recent years, psychology has been telling us that our choices are more compulsive than we realize. John Calvin referred to this as depravity. Jesus called it slavery to sin. The only way to get free of it is to confess it, to tell the truth about our need for a Savior.

That means freedom is not a matter of what we know, but whom we know; it has nothing to do with our achievements, and everything to do with what Christ has already achieved for us.

The Truth Rises

"Nothing is hidden that will not be disclosed, nor is anything secret that will not become known and come to light."
Luke 8:17

READ LUKE 8:16-18

Have you ever tried to hold a beach ball under water? Eventually you get tired of the effort, and the ball rises to the surface. The truth is buoyant like that. It is possible to hide it for a while, but that takes a lot of effort. In time, the truth always emerges.

The good news in this is that you don't have to spend a lot of energy defending yourself against rumors and lies. It is possible to waste so much time explaining what you didn't do that you have precious little time for the things you really want to do. When you hear that someone is saying things that are not true, relax. In time, the truth will rise to the surface.

The bad news in this is that if you are trying to hide the truth about yourself, you are fighting a losing battle. Protecting a secret is exhausting work, and in the end, the truth will still come out.

Rather than managing our sins, our only hope is to confess them. In confession we give up control of our sins. We take our hands off the ball and give it to Jesus, who can then tell us that we are forgiven. The word *forgive* in the New Testament means to make free. To be forgiven is to be freed to get on with life because we are no longer preoccupied with controlling the past.

❦

Accept the Forgiveness, Receive the Love

"The one to whom little is forgiven, loves little."

Luke 7:47

Read Luke 7:36-50

A Pharisee named Simon was having dinner with Jesus when a woman who was known to be a sinner appeared out of nowhere. She knelt at Jesus' feet, bathed his feet with her tears, and dried them with her hair. Then she kissed and anointed Jesus' feet with expensive ointment. Simon was unimpressed and wondered why Jesus let this sinner even touch him.

So Jesus told a story about two people who owed a creditor more money than they could pay. One owed five hundred days' wages and the other owed fifty. In mercy, the creditor canceled both debts. "So, Simon," Jesus asked, "Who do you think will love him more?" Jesus did not tell Simon this story to teach us that you have to become a big sinner to receive God's forgiveness. He told the story to say that the more you tell the truth about your need to be forgiven, the more you'll fall in love with God.

Both a Pharisee and a sinner live inside each of us. None of us is all bad or all good. We tend to show God only the Pharisee, while hiding the sinner, who lurks in the shadows of our hearts. Yet we can never hide him deep enough. The sinner in us keeps reappearing to tear down what the Pharisee has built up. God doesn't just love our good side. God loves us—all of us. If we want to discover more of that love we have to accept more of his forgiveness, and we can't do that until we tell more of the truth.

❦

Friends and Forgiveness

When Jesus saw their faith, he said to the paralytic, "Son, your sins are forgiven."

Mark 2:5

READ MARK 2:1-12

The crowd was so enormous at the house where Jesus was staying that some men cut a hole in the roof and lowered their paralyzed friend down in front of him. There comes a time for all of us when we are paralyzed by fear or anger, grief or confusion. A real friend will avoid the temptation to give us advice. That would be like giving tips on walking to a paralyzed person. What we need at times like that is for someone simply to carry us to Jesus in prayer.

We are told that when Jesus saw their faith, he healed the sick man. Frequently in the Bible someone is healed because of the faith of someone else. Certainly, each of us needs to nurture faith in our lives, but we will never have enough on our own. Especially when we are paralyzed, we need to lean upon the faith of others.

In saying, "Your sins are forgiven," Jesus was not saying that all sickness is caused by sin. Yet he was saying that what we all really need is forgiveness for our sin-sick souls. That is because nothing can cripple like guilt, and it is the hardest thing to heal. This means that after they carry us to Jesus, the other thing we need from our friends is absolution. There are so many things we have to do for ourselves in the Christian life. Yet when it comes to forgiveness, we need a friend who will be our priest, reminding us, "In Jesus Christ, you are forgiven."

❦

Remember His Grace

Remember these things.... I have swept away your transgressions like a cloud, and your sins like mist; return to me, for I have redeemed you.

Isaiah 44:21-22

READ ISAIAH 44:21-23

It is striking how often the Bible tells us to remember. We are told to remember God's faithfulness that has brought us through the great waters and fiery trials of our past, and thus we will not lose hope when the day is hard. We are told to remember that we are part of a people of faith whose story with God started long before we got to our chapter, and thus we work for a dream that outlives us. We are told to remember that in the Holy Scriptures God has revealed our way of life, and thus we will always be distinctive from those who live by different norms and expectations. We are told to remember all these things, because they are important to living in a world where it is easy to get confused about who we are.

One thing that we are never told to remember is our confessed sin. That is because God has already forgotten about it. In fact, he has swept it away "like mist."

It is striking that while we have such a hard time remembering things like God's faithfulness, we find it very easy to remember our past sins, and the sins of those who have hurt us. We forget what we should remember. We can't let go of the things we should forget. I'm not sure why that is, but my fear is that we will never be able to remember his grace as long we are cherishing our sins.

❦

Facing the Truth

For the wrath of God is revealed from heaven against all ungodliness and wickedness of those who by their wickedness suppress the truth.

Romans 1:18

READ ROMANS 1:16-32

Most of us don't want to think about the wrath of God. We prefer his love. Yet the opposite of wrath is not love. It's remaining neutral. And God loves you too much to be neutral about your life. His wrath is that of a lover's quarrel, for he can't remain silent while you hurt yourself.

According to the apostle Paul, one way to make God furious is to suppress the truth. The only way to cover up sin and failure is with more sin and failure. Not only does this hurt our souls, but it isn't even effective. The truth is buoyant and eventually rises to the surface.

In the first two chapters of Romans, however, Paul is worried about an even more egregious suppression of truth. That is the deadly effort at covering up the truth God has written onto our hearts. He claims we don't even have to read the Bible to know that some things are simply wrong. It's wrong to be immoral, to hurt others, or to waste life with self-indulgence. In spite of all the contemporary protestations to the contrary, we all know that in our hearts. That's because God loved us enough to give us a conscience.

Your conscience can't save you. It will just illustrate how much trouble you are in. For salvation, you'll have to accept God's forgiveness, but you won't be able to do that until you first listen to the hard truth rising up from your heart.

❦

The Evil Within Us

"Judas, is it with a kiss that you are betraying the Son of Man?"

Luke 22:48

Read Luke 22:47-53

We have always reserved our greatest judgment for those who betray us. That's because it shatters not only our faith in the person who hurt us but also our faith in the whole idea of trust. Betrayal is one of those gifts that just keeps giving. It hurts all of our relationships.

That is why we are very hard on Judas in the biblical narrative. Yet could it be that our real reason for showing him so little compassion is that we are afraid there is a betrayal chromosome in us? I think we fear Judas more than we do the cross. The cross is a symbol of heroic self-sacrifice, but Judas is a symbol of the evil within us.

At the Last Supper, when Jesus claimed that one of the twelve would betray him, the fragility of all of their relationships with him was revealed when each said, "Surely it is not I, Lord?" It was as if they were each saying, "I have worried about that, but I was sure I had it under control." So we take it out on Judas. The sin that is always most difficult to forgive in another is the one with which we struggle in our own lives. No one is as merciless as those who have no mercy on their own evil.

As the passion of Christ unfolded, the real tragedy of Judas' life was not that he betrayed Jesus but that he destroyed himself with guilt once he realized what he had done. He was therefore not there by the cross when Jesus said, "Father, forgive."

۴

To Be Made Right

Have mercy upon us, O Lord, have mercy upon us, for we have had more than enough of contempt.

Psalm 123:3

READ PSALM 123

It seems that most of us don't really need to be convinced that we are sinners. We are pretty clear about that. What we doubt is that we can find mercy. That's because there is so little of it in the world.

Even our secular society has great contempt for sinners. We judge people harshly for their transgressions, failures, and mistakes. Ironically, we even judge others for being judgmental. Yet the worst judge of all is the one who shows up in the mirror each morning. We are never satisfied with what we see in ourselves. So when we hear about the merciful God, it confuses us.

The mercy of God doesn't mean there is no judgment for our sins. It means that in Christ, the judge was judged in our place. The harsh world is half right. There is always a price to be paid for our sin. Yet on the cross, that price has already been paid. We are forgiven.

To be forgiven means to be free. You are free from managing your sins, a practice that leads only to more sin. You are free from judging yourself and accepting the judgments of others. Best of all, however, you are free from continuing to sin. So to ask for God's mercy is not simply to ask for a break from all the judgment. It is to ask to be changed, made right, until your life will start to look like the holy life of Jesus.

SEVEN

Meeting God in Prayer

❦

Believing in God, Not Prayer

While Peter was kept in prison, the church prayed fervently to God for him.

Acts 12:5

READ ACTS 12:1-17

When King Herod saw how happy he made people by arresting and killing James, he also arrested Peter, intending to kill him as well. So the Church began to pray fervently for Peter. During the night, an angel came and quietly helped Peter escape from jail. Peter went to the home where the Church was gathered in prayer for him. When he knocked at the gate of the home, a servant named Rhoda was startled to see him. She left Peter at the gate and ran back into the house to tell the Church that he was outside. They said, "You are out of your mind," and returned to their prayers for his release.

It was easier for the Church to pray than to believe God would answer their prayers. I understand that. Sometimes I also pray as a discipline, yet doubt that anything will really change. The Church probably prayed for James' release as well, but he was still killed by Herod. So why should they believe that the Lord would answer their prayers for Peter?

This is a good question, but it's really beside the point when it comes to prayer, which is not a prescription for getting what we want. We don't actually believe in prayer. We believe in God, to whom we pray. We pray simply to be with God, which is more important than telling him what we want. When we are anxious about something, what we really need is to know God is with us, and that is something we can receive every time we ask. It is enough.

❦

The Key to Everything Else

Have salt in yourselves.

Mark 9:50

Read Mark 9:49-50

Jesus told us to be salty not only because he wants his followers to be distinctive but also because he expects us to have character. Nothing makes Jesus nuts quite like milquetoast disciples who think they are spiritual when they are actually just boring. The purpose of his ministry among us was to forgive our sins and restore us to being fully alive. So you cannot receive the amazing grace of Jesus without becoming rather amazing yourself.

If you want to know what this looks like, pay close attention to Jesus' own life. He loved dinner parties and preferred to go to those with a few disreputable people in attendance. If the wine ran out, well, you remember what happened at Cana. Yet Jesus also had the ability to break down in tears when he saw the pathos for which Jerusalem was headed, and that is still the only rational response to the pathos of Jerusalem today. He had a soft spot for children, blue-collar workers, and anyone in trouble, but he didn't mind unmasking the sin of those who considered themselves righteous. He loved the masses but didn't mind being alone, and periodically chose to go to "a lonely place" to find solitude with his heavenly Father.

This last thing may be the key to everything else about Jesus, and the salty character he expects of you. When you learn how to find solitude with the Father, you are renewed in your true identity as the beloved. People who know they are loved cannot help but be fully alive.

❦

Heaven Responds

This is the victory that conquers the world, our faith.

1 John 5:4

READ 1 JOHN 5:1-5

Most ancient religions believed the affairs of humanity were directly determined by the actions of the gods. If the gods were happy, things went well on earth. If they were angry, well, you had better duck. In fact, natural phenomena were explained as being the by-product of the actions of the fickle gods above us. Lightning, earthquakes, and floods were the result of the gods' anger. Sunshine, spring, and rainbows were the result of their pleasure.

The New Testament turns this thesis upside down by placing incredible power in the hands of humans. It even claims that heaven is affected by the choices we make. Whenever a believer prays, we are told that heaven responds. When a sinner repents, heaven rejoices. When a believer turns from Christ, it is the Holy Spirit who is grieved. When we cast out demonic evil, Satan is limited. Jesus' promise that we would receive the power of the Holy Spirit wasn't just some metaphor. We really do have the power of God to make changes.

Perhaps the strange condition of our world today is directly related to our careless use of the power we have. Like the ancient gods before us, we are fickle and self-absorbed. This is as good an explanation as any for the very natural phenomena of hate and greed.

All of this is to say that our prayers make a great deal of difference to God. Apparently they also make a great deal of difference to our life on earth. We bring heaven and earth closer together with our prayers.

❦

The Wholeness of God

Now we see in a mirror dimly, but then we will see face to face.

1 Corinthians 13:12

READ 1 CORINTHIANS 13

What we think about ourselves is probably more related to what we think about God than most of us realize. Theologian Paul Tillich called God "the ground of our being." God is the foundation upon which life is built. If your foundation is flawed, the rest of life's structure is going to be pretty shaky.

For example, those of us who have a hard time living joyfully probably live with an angry and judgmental God. Those who have difficulty with control issues may think God is rather demanding. If you struggle to believe that people really love you, it's a good bet that your God-image is not very nurturing. I seem to struggle an awful lot with the absence of God, and wonder why he so often leaves things undone. That probably has a lot to do with my fears that I won't accomplish enough with my life.

It is as if we see God through very dark glasses that distort our perceptions of the rest of the world as well. That is why worship is so important for us. For as we encounter the glory of God, like Paul, we are blinded by the realization that there is more to God than we know. He strips away the dark glasses and forces us to see the truth—about him, and then about ourselves. If we keep encountering the true character of God, in time our understanding will begin to reflect the wholeness of God.

❦

Prayer in Success

But he would withdraw to deserted places and pray.

Luke 5:16

READ LUKE 5:12-16

By the time we get to the fifth chapter of Luke's Gospel, Jesus' popularity was at an all-time high. He had been healing, preaching, and casting out demons. Every day the number of people following him grew larger and larger. So it's striking that immediately after describing Jesus' great success, the very next thing Luke tells us is, "but he would withdraw to deserted places to pray."

Most of us are pretty good about praying when things are not going well. When people we care about are having a hard time, they appreciate hearing us say, "I'll pray for you." Yet I wonder if that is also true when they are successful. A friend tells you, "I just got my dream job!" Imagine responding, "Really? I'll pray for you." It sounds funny, but as Jesus knew, it's during our moments of success that we most need prayer. That's because success is more dangerous to our spirituality than failure. When we're approved of by others, we don't spend as much time on our knees seeking God's approval. Nothing can dry up our spirits as quickly.

It is also significant that Jesus withdrew to deserted places to pray. Where you pray is very important. Apparently, it needs to be a place where you have deserted your success long enough to remember the truth—it's all a gift from God. That will make it easier to give back the success someday. As Jesus can tell you, that day's coming, and you'll survive it only if you believe you're still approved of by God.

✤

Sufficient Grace

"My grace is sufficient for you, for my power is made perfect in weakness."

2 Corinthians 12:9

READ 2 CORINTHIANS 12:1-10

God did not become human that we might become gods, but that we might become more fully human. God alone is whole and complete, lacking in nothing. Creatures, by contrast, always seem to have some mark of dependency, some painful grace, that keeps them close to their Creator. That is because brokenness is an essential characteristic of being human. It is also our best opportunity to live with a Savior.

Only in recent years, with our fascination over individual wholeness, have we assumed that our humanity is not supposed to have any chips, blemishes, or bruises on it. Now, we even think we have a right to have it all—perfect health, perfect relationships, perfect job satisfaction, and grief-free living. Yet perfection is not the biblical depiction of creatures.

The Bible describes us as a people who need a Savior. There is no time when that is more obvious than when our dreams for life break apart. Certainly, we have been encouraged to pray for healing, but God's response may have little to do with our need to get life all fixed up.

The apostle Paul described a "thorn in the flesh" that he had asked God to remove. In spite of repeated petitions the thorn remained, and Paul learned a great deal about the sufficiency of God's grace. That doesn't mean that God teaches us to put up with the thorns. It means that the hurts in life become our best altars for worshiping God, which is the point of life.

❦

Blessed Insecurity

"Come, let us build ourselves a city, and a tower with its top in the heavens, and let us make a name for ourselves."

Genesis 11:4

READ GENESIS 11:1-9

These days we are saturated with information. By picking up a newspaper, you can learn incredible details on the inner workings of small Eastern European governments. CNN can take you around the world in thirty minutes. We confront hundreds of advertisements, memos, and messages in the course of a day. Through the Internet we can now receive so much information that we could never process everything we can "download"—and I do love that word.

The amazing thing is that most of us feel uninformed. That makes us insecure, because in our society knowledge is power. Information gives us the power to make decisions, the power to hold others accountable, and the power to pursue our dreams. Perhaps it is for this reason that being informed has now become something of a right for us.

I wonder if maybe we aren't getting close to crossing a line that separates creatures from the Creator. We once tried to secure power through building a tower called Babel. Then we looked for power in the idols of wood and stone. Soon we graduated to kings and armies, nations and empires, and even a powerful Church. More recently, we have tried to secure our lives through industry, science, and wealth. And still, we feel insecure. Will Microsoft really change that for us?

Maybe we were meant to feel some insecurity. Maybe that is God's invitation to worship him, who alone creates our lives.

❧

Humbled in Prayer

The Lord said, "See, he has hidden himself among the baggage."

1 Samuel 10:22

READ 1 SAMUEL 10:17-27

When he was young, Saul didn't want to be king. When the lot fell to him, he even hid, hoping he could escape the call to leadership. Yet the Lord has a way of getting what he wants, so he told everyone exactly where Saul was hiding. Maybe it was because Saul felt inadequate, or because he had other plans for his life, but clearly the young man was a very reluctant leader.

All good leaders are reluctant. That isn't just because they have counted the high cost. More importantly, it is because they have no personal need to be in leadership. Yet those are exactly the people God always chooses. If you need to be in leadership, you're of little use to God because you will do anything to stay in leadership. You'll even stop listening to God.

That's how Saul later got into great trouble, and it's how our leaders get into trouble as well. If we can't walk away from leadership, we are not serving God, who alone is the necessary leader. We are not necessary. That's true for politicians, CEOs, teachers, and clergy. It's also true for parents, who have to let their children leave home.

We have no record of Saul ever throwing himself before the Lord in prayer. The only times he worshiped were when he wanted God to do something for him. He never asked God to do anything to him, to change his character, or to make him a man after God's own heart. So God found another leader.

❦

Break the Silence

And a voice from heaven said, "This is my Son, the Beloved, with whom I am well pleased."

Matthew 3:17

READ MATTHEW 3:1-17

It is striking how much God talks at the beginning of the Bible. Over and over we read, "God said let there be ... and there was..." Through the later part of the Bible, however, it seems God's words are much harder to come by. Perhaps that is because once we started listening to the words of the serpent, it became harder to hear the voice of our Creator.

Thankfully, there came a time when God couldn't let the silence go any further. Eventually, he had to rip back the skies to say, "This is my Son, the Beloved." Unless you have grown accustomed to the silence of God, it is hard to remember why the arrival of Jesus was such good news. As the Christ, Jesus is the embodiment of God's longing to start talking with us again. Not at us, but with us.

Remember when you were young and you would have done anything to hear your father say that he was pleased with you? That is exactly what we hear from the heavenly Father. In submitting to John's baptism for sinners, Jesus identified himself with us. In Jesus Christ, God has said all he can about his love for us. If our relationships with him still seem pretty quiet, it's because we're not talking back.

Prayer is a breaking of the silence between us and God. As with any lover, we can whisper, chat, cry, or even argue with God. Yet we dare not settle for silence. Not after God has said so much.

❦

Doubters Encouraged to Apply

When they saw [Jesus], they worshiped him; but some doubted.

Matthew 28:17

READ MATTHEW 28:16-20

This verse immediately precedes the Great Commission when Jesus sent his disciples into all the world. By this time Jesus' followers had seen him do many miraculous things. The hungry had been fed and the sick had been healed. Jesus had even risen from the dead. So how could some of the disciples still have had doubts? How could Jesus have given even the doubters the responsibility of finishing the mission he began?

It seems that the point of the passage is that even though some of the disciples doubted, all of them worshiped Jesus. That is what is expected of every disciple. Actually, we, too, have seen the faithfulness of Jesus, and yet some of us still have our doubts as well. It is not that we doubt his power. Usually what we doubt is that he will be powerful in our lives. According to the gospel, however, Jesus doesn't seem to be worried about these doubts, as long as we still worship.

When we worship, we lose ourselves at the feet of the Savior. That means we lose our certainties as well as our doubts. Jesus is not impressed by our faith, and he is not dismayed by our doubts. What matters to Jesus is our love. That is why we worship. Even though we don't always understand him, we know that we do love this man whose passion for us took him to the cross. Of course, it is that love that then propels us into mission.

❦

Asking in the Name of Jesus

"Very truly, I tell you, if you ask anything of the Father in my name, he will give it to you."

John 16:23

READ JOHN 16:16-28

This verse contains a rather impressive promise. My guess is that it seems a little too impressive to most of us. For some the problem is that the image of the earthly father gets in the way. I was always frightened to ask for things from my father. I loved my parents and knew they didn't have much money. Rather than making them feel bad about not being able to give more to their sons, it was easier just to go without the things I wanted. So, I often forget that my heavenly Father can give me whatever he wants. I assume that God is just doing the best he can. This is a realistic view of our dads, but a diminished view of God.

For others the problem is that the image of being an earthly child gets in the way. Remember, it is only if we ask in the name of Jesus that we receive. That means we must ask for things as if the Son of God were asking the Father himself. I may want a new house or car, but those aren't the things Jesus tended to bring to his Father in prayer. This doesn't mean that they will never come, but they are clearly beyond the scope of what is promised. Typically the things Jesus asked of the Father had little to do with Jesus and everything to do with what he wanted for others. So maybe the starting place for our prayers is to ask, most of all, to become like Jesus.

꙳

God's Will: A Grateful Heart

Go, eat your bread with enjoyment, and drink your wine with a merry heart; for God has long ago approved what you do.

Ecclesiastes 9:7

READ ECCLESIASTES 9:7-9

I find that when people say they want to talk to me about discerning God's will, we almost always end up discussing their struggle in finding the right job. Since we spend a lot of time at work, it makes sense that we want to be sure it's the right job for us. The assumption we have is that if we are doing what God wants us to do, then we will be happy. That also means that if we aren't happy, we must not be doing the will of God. Yet I wonder sometimes if God is as worried as we are about what we do for a job.

It's a particularly American tendency to reduce the will of God to a job description. Yet the Bible speaks much more specifically about God's will for our character than it does about his will for our jobs. It may be that God's will is no more complicated than glorifying and enjoying him forever. If you can do that in your present job, great. If you want to quit and get another job, go ahead. Unless you're planning on working for the mob, God is probably going to bless your work no matter who is signing your checks. Yet that is not the real issue.

We should be much more concerned about whether we are developing a grateful heart along the way. Giving thanks, we know, is the will of God. It's a sign of spiritual character.

❦

God's Sovereignty, Our Freedom

I have made, and I will bear; I will carry and will save.

Isaiah 46:4

READ ISAIAH 46:1-13

The Bible places great stress upon the sovereignty of God, who alone is in control of our lives and the destiny of this world. This does not rob humans of responsibility, but it does change the things for which we have responsibility. Rather than being preoccupied with making a good life for ourselves, we who believe in the sovereignty of God are quite concerned about receiving the life he is trying to give us.

For example, people who really believe that God is in control do not try to manage the future. That is not because they are unconcerned about the future. They pray about it often. Yet in prayer they are reminded that only God is capable of creating the future. That makes it easier to leave tomorrow in his hands.

Similarly, the doctrine of God's sovereignty frees Christians from living with regret, or with an obsession to redeem the past. Our job is simply to confess our failures. When we give the past back to God, we usually discover great purpose and meaning in what we thought was just an awful experience. With a sovereign God, nothing is wasted.

That means that what Christians need most to do is to worship and give thanks to God for his salvation. If you find your desire for worship is low, that may be a sign that you are still enslaved by the illusion that you can make your past or your future right without God.

❦

Prayers to Bring Us Home

Jesus offered up prayers and supplications with loud cries and tears.

Hebrews 5:7

READ HEBREWS 5:1-14

Often when we are having hard times, someone will say, "I'll pray for you." We always respond by saying, "Thanks." I've never had anyone, even an agnostic, become offended when I've offered to pray for him or her. We may not know what those prayers will accomplish, but we do appreciate the effort.

What if it were Jesus Christ who offered to pray for you? How would you react then? My guess is that you would respond with something stronger than, "Thanks." Maybe it would be more along the lines of, "Really?" And you would expect those prayers to be answered because, after all, you would have the Son of God praying for you now. Yet you might want to listen in on what Jesus is saying when he prays for you. Nowhere in the Bible are we told that Jesus will ask God to prevent us from having hard times. What we are told is that he will forgive our sins and bring us home to his Father.

The author of Hebrews claims that Jesus is our Great High Priest. Like a priest, Jesus hears our confession and grants absolution. Yet priests don't change our circumstances. What they change is our relationship to God. When it comes to that, Jesus prays "with loud cries and tears."

Once you are in the right relationship with God, you no longer will allow the hard times to define you. You will still have them, but you just won't value them so much.

❧

His Yoke Is Easy

"Come to me, all you that are weary and are carrying heavy burdens, and I will give you rest. Take my yoke upon you."
Matthew 11:28-29

READ MATTHEW 11:28-30

It is ironic that after Jesus promises to give rest to all who weary of carrying heavy burdens, he then tells us to take his yoke upon our shoulders. The reason we should do this, he says, is because his yoke is easy and his burden is light. This means that if you're tired of carrying the heavy burdens of family, work, or health, then the only way to find rest is to take on the burdens of the Savior of the world, because those are lighter than the ones you are carrying around. Hmm.

Maybe the point here is that no one finds rest simply by getting rid of burdens. According to Jesus, rest comes from bearing the right burdens.

Most of the concerns we lug around through life were not placed on our shoulders by God. Maybe they were given to us by others who manipulated our addiction to pleasing people. More probably, we have picked up these burdens on our own because we are trying too hard to get life just right. Wherever it came from, if a burden doesn't feel light, then it didn't come from Jesus. The reason Christ's yoke is easy is because we are constantly reminded that these are his burdens we are bearing. So rather than fix things, we just use his yoke to carry our concerns back to him. All of this means that the yoke of Christ, your calling at home and work, is best seen as a way of praying.

❦

Living Water for Thirsty Souls

I remember your name in the night, O Lord, and keep your law.

Psalm 119:55

Read Psalm 119:49-56

Most of the things we do to hurt our relationship to God happen during the night. Maybe that is because by the evening we are tired, hurt, and disappointed in the day we have finished. We've been good all day, and it hasn't done a thing for us. So in our anger we do things that hurt others, ourselves, and the image of God within us.

There is another, deeper, reason for our sins of the evening. By the end of the day we've run out of work and are now having to find other ways to distract ourselves from the insatiable thirst of our parched souls. It doesn't matter how much of a workaholic you are, you can stay busy with productivity for only so long. When you have to put your day job aside and confront that thirsty soul, you are left with a great choice. You can try to numb the soul by abusing alcohol, sex, or the shopping channel. Or, as the psalmist tells us, you can remember the name of the Lord.

The next time you are exhausted and depleted at the end of the day, try simply saying the name "Lord Jesus Christ." Say it over and over. Meditate on it. Sing it in a hymn. You'll be amazed at the power of that name. According to the Bible, it can make the devil flee. More importantly, Jesus cannot resist coming to those who call on him. When he comes, he always brings his living water for our thirsty souls.

EIGHT

Rooted in Faith

*

Jesus Will Complete You

Looking to Jesus, the pioneer and perfecter of our faith.

Hebrews 12:2

READ HEBREWS 12:1-13

Living by faith is not easy. Every day confronts you with another reason to doubt that God loves you and has a future for you filled with hope. Sometimes you wonder how that could be true. The author of Hebrews reminds us that your faith is first of all our faith. It isn't just something you have to keep alive. It is there when you feel like you have it, and it is still there when you don't, because faith belongs to us, the Church. In the times when you can't really keep your end up, there are others who can hold the faith until you can get your hands on it again.

We are also told that Jesus is the pioneer and perfecter of our faith. As the pioneer, he has already entered every home, office, and school before we get there in the morning. He has already faced every temptation we are going to encounter in the course of the day. Nothing harsh will be said to us that has not already been said to him. We are never alone. And since Jesus is also the perfecter of our faith, it's OK for us to be less than perfect as Christians. He will complete what we leave undone. The important thing is not that we learn to succeed as Christians, but that we learn to accept his love and mercy.

❦

Believing Is Seeing

Jesus came and stood among them.... He showed them his
hands and his side. Then the disciples rejoiced.

John 20:19-20

READ JOHN 20:19-29

When Jesus found the disciples, they were hiding behind the doors of the Upper Room. It was not until they saw the ugly marks on his hands and side that their fear turned to joy. Later, Thomas, who missed this appearance, also demanded to see the wounds before he could believe.

What is it about these marks? They are the wounds of the cross. The marks of being forgiven. To see them is to discover that the thing you feared the most—that there is a limit to God's grace—well, you were wrong about it. All is forgiven, and people who believe they are forgiven have little to fear in life.

Once Thomas finally saw the wounded risen Christ, he said, "My Lord and my God!" Jesus responded by telling him that the real blessing comes to those who believe without having to see. When we read that, we are tempted to say, "Yes, maybe, but I would still trade places with Thomas. I would love to see for myself."

Why is there a blessing for those who believe without having seen? Because their doubts are not taken away. The only place for their faith to grow is in the midst of their doubts. The opposite of faith is not doubt, but fear. Most of the time doubt is the mother of faith.

The Bible doesn't tell us not to doubt. It tells us news that is worthy of doubt, that is too good to be true: "Fear not. You have been forgiven."

❦

An Unfulfilled Hunger

"One does not live by bread alone."

Luke 4:4

READ LUKE 4:1-13

We are such a hungry people. It is even in our created design to wake up every morning confronted with appetite. We have been blessed, I think, to live in a society in which most of our appetites are easily filled. We have food, homes, friends, medical care, money, and even the luxury to wonder what we would prefer to do for a living. Yet, we hunger for more. The human capacity for unhappiness is enormous. It's a black hole that we can never fill.

All of this hunger confronts us with a choice. Will our insatiable appetites become our god, or will we see this hunger as a yearning for the true God? Yearning for God is not the same thing as yearning for more of God's material blessings. There comes a time when we realize that even our instrumental use for God is unsatisfying.

Imagine what life would be like if you received everything you asked for from God. You wouldn't have any needs, or heartaches, or uncertainty. You also wouldn't have any faith. Who needs faith if God rushes in to grant every request? Faith is a choice to stay with God in spite of your unfulfilled hunger.

Why is your faith so important to God? Because it's the only thing that binds loving relationships together. God wants a loving relationship with you more than he wants to satisfy you. That's a good thing, because once you get to the bottom of your hunger, you'll discover that loving God was what you wanted all along.

❧

A Time to Carry and a Time to Be Carried

"Stand up, take your bed, and go to your home."

Matthew 9:6

READ MATTHEW 9:1-8

Matthew tells us that one day "some people" carried a paralyzed man to Jesus. When Jesus saw their faith, he healed the man they were carrying. Notice how passive the paralyzed man is through all of this. He is carried to Jesus by some people who are so anonymous in the story that we aren't even given their names. Yet it was because of their faith that Jesus healed the man.

Sooner or later, something is going to happen to you that leaves your faith weak. You will be unable to get to Jesus by yourself. Then you'll have to let others carry you with their faith. This is what people are doing when they say, "I'm praying for you." They realize they can't be your Savior, so they don't interject their advice or personality into the story. Instead they just become some people who carry you to the Healer in prayer. Jesus can never resist that level of faith.

Eventually, Jesus will tell you that it is now time to stand on your own feet, and return to the business of life. This is when your own faith has to come back to life. You don't have to believe in order to be healed by Jesus, but you do if you want to enjoy the healing. The most faithful thing you can do is to know when to stop being paralyzed by your hurt and grief. You will know when that time has come because you will then be more interested in carrying others than in being carried.

❦

The Real Question

"Rabbi, who sinned, this man or his parents, that he was born blind?"

John 9:2

READ JOHN 9:1-41

Trying to encourage class participation, a teacher will sometimes say, "There are no bad questions." Maybe, but there are certainly ineffectual ones. The point of a question is to solicit an answer, and until we find the right question, we will never find the right answer to the most troubling riddles of life.

The disciples once asked Jesus whose sin was responsible for a man being born blind. It's the kind of question we ponder as well. Who is responsible for my problems? Whom should I blame? Or sue? Yet those questions will never help us find salvation. Even if we find someone to blame, we still haven't done anything about the problem. In fact, we've probably made it worse. Unless it leads to forgiveness, assigning blame only turns the blamer into a victim.

The real question, Jesus said, was not who was responsible for the man's blindness but who could heal him? Then, restoring the man's vision, Jesus said, "He was born blind so that God's works may be revealed in him." We are not always healed of our diseases, but if we pray for the vision, we can always see God at work in our brokenness. Seeing that God is with us, we can discover how to find healing for our broken, angry souls.

Why would you settle for being a victim knowing whom to blame, when you can be healed knowing whom to praise?

❦

God of the Big Things, God of the Small Things

"Where are we to get enough bread in the desert to feed so great a crowd?"

Matthew 15:33

Read Matthew 15:32-38

This is the question that the disciples asked when Jesus indicated that he wanted to feed four thousand people. Normally, the question would make sense. Yet the way Matthew tells the story, this happened not many days after Jesus had miraculously fed five thousand people. It was as if the disciples were saying, "Sure, he can feed five thousand, but can he feed four thousand?" So the question doesn't make sense after all. No, but it is believable.

As strange as it sounds, we have a lot of trouble believing in "the smaller miracle." Most of us don't have that much difficulty believing that God created the heavens and the earth, but we certainly have our doubts that he is still creating a good work in our lives. We don't really doubt that the Savior Jesus was raised from the dead, but we struggle to believe that he can pull us out of our tombs of despair and heartache. To put it more accurately, we believe God could save our lives but we doubt he will.

When you limit God's miracles to the bigger events, you are essentially saying that he is not really God, but only another distant force of nature. To truly believe in him is to believe that he is the Savior of your life. If you believe God wants the sun to stay in the sky, then does it really make sense to doubt that he also wants to bring the light of salvation to you?

꽃

Footlights ... Not Floodlights

Your word is a lamp to my feet and a light to my path.
Psalm 119:105

Read Psalm 119:105-112

The Bible is God's Word to us. That means it can't be reduced to a science text. Science is worried about the questions why, how, and when. The Bible is concerned about who. It is not a history, literature, or political text. The Bible is the unfolding mystery of God's drama in our lives. Like any good mystery, it gives us only enough information to keep us going.

The psalmist compares God's Word to a footlight. Notice, he doesn't call it an enormous floodlight. That's what we would have preferred—lots of light so we could see everything for the next fifty years. Yet if we were given that much light, it would scare us to death, so thank God that all we have been given are those little foot lamps that line the walkway. It's just enough light to stay on track.

Sometimes the Bible tells us things that are confusing, but that's because the path of life hasn't yet taken us to a place where that message makes a lot of sense. That really isn't the hard part. Mark Twain once said that it wasn't the parts of the Bible he didn't understand that bothered him, but the parts he did. It's all the struggle we can handle to be faithful to what we do understand in God's Word. Yet as we continue to struggle with its painfully clear light, we will eventually discover that light revealing a Savior on the path with us.

❦

How to Amaze Jesus

"Only speak the word, and let my servant be healed. For I am also a man set under authority...." When Jesus heard this he was amazed.

Luke 7:7-9

READ LUKE 7:1-10

Once Jesus encountered a centurion who asked him simply to give an order so his servant would be healed. Jesus was amazed and said he had never seen that much faith. The faith that Jesus found so amazing was not that the centurion believed his servant would be healed, but that he had the faith to place himself under the authority of the Savior.

The centurion's faith was not in what he wanted to have happen. His faith was in Jesus, whatever happened.

To be truly under the authority of Jesus means that we continue to believe him, even when we do not understand him. The centurion's servant was healed. Yet how do we explain all the other people of Palestine in Jesus' day whose loved ones were not healed? How do we explain the deaths of those who slip away from us in spite of all our sincere prayers? We can't always explain Jesus. If we could, he would be under our authority.

Sometimes we believe because of what Jesus does. Sometimes we believe in spite of what he does. Trust has its reasons and its wounds. As in any relationship, we choose to trust only because we love the person we are trusting. We love because of, and in spite of. Yet we don't have to understand.

That kind of faith is rare. So rare that it amazes even Jesus.

❦

The Danger of a Little Faith

"Take heart, it is I; do not be afraid."

Matthew 14:27

READ MATTHEW 14:22-33

The disciples had just been through a hard night, fighting a strong wind on their boat. Early the next morning, while the storm was still raging, they looked across the water and saw Jesus walking toward them. Peter then said, "Lord, if it is you, command me to come to you on the water." And Jesus said, "Come."

Things started out well enough for Peter as he left the boat and walked toward his Savior. Yet then he felt the strong wind, and it occurred to him that he couldn't walk on water. At that point he began to sink and cried out for Jesus to save him.

After pulling Peter out of the water, Jesus said, "You of little faith, why did you doubt?" I've always thought those words were a bit harsh. Why didn't Jesus chastise the other disciples who stayed in the boat? At least Peter gave it a try, and he almost made it. Yes, he almost made it, but not quite. Before he got to Jesus, Peter turned his eyes back to the things that made him afraid.

Jesus has always been hardest on those who have little faith, and he doesn't tolerate their fears of the wind that is against them. Frankly, Jesus is harder on people with a little faith than he is on those who have no faith at all. That is because even with some faith, you have seen enough of Jesus to walk toward him. And after you have seen the Savior, why would you be afraid?

❦

Fear at the Service of Faith

Happy are those who fear the Lord.

Psalm 112:1

READ PSALM 112

There is no shortage of reasons to be afraid in this life. Some people fear their past. Maybe they are haunted by past mistakes and now worry that those mistakes have put a lien on their dreams. The reason we fear our past is because we have no power to change it.

Others are afraid of the unpredictable future. They cannot be certain that what they desperately want to happen will happen, nor can they be certain that what they dread will not happen. We have always feared the things we cannot control, and the future is as hard to control as the past.

Even if we just focus on the present we have plenty of opportunities to fear. We can fear the loss of our health, money, jobs, reputations, dreams, cherished loved ones, and the list goes on and on. Eventually we will lose all of these things. The fear is that we may lose them today. So not even the present is in our control.

The only way out of all this anxiety is to fear God. We don't fear God because we worry he will hurt us, but because he loves us so incredibly much. Sacred love is also uncontrollable. You can't be certain how God will demonstrate his love, and that's frightening. Yet if you don't fear God you'll fear everything else in life. If you do fear God you won't fear anything else, because nothing in the past, present, or future is beyond the power of the God who loves you.

❦

Just Keep Following

"Lord, to whom can we go? You have the words of eternal life."

John 6:68

READ JOHN 6:60-71

Although we are most familiar with the twelve disciples, the gospels make it clear that early in Jesus' ministry there were many people who were following him. They all had high hopes for what this new leader would do. Jesus, however, was not easily swayed by what the crowd wanted to hear. Some of the things he said were hard to believe. Other things he said were simply hard to understand.

In John 6:66-67 we are told, "Because of this, many of his disciples turned back and no longer went about with him. So Jesus asked the twelve, 'Do you also wish to go away?'" I expected that the twelve would have taken this moment to shine as star disciples who say, "No, Jesus, we understand you perfectly and are 100 percent behind your vision for ministry." Yet they couldn't say that. They didn't understand Jesus any better than those who left him did. All they could say was, "Lord, to whom can we go? You have the words of eternal life." The real disciples of Jesus Christ may not always understand his words but they believe they are the truest words they will ever hear. Maybe they are even too true to be easily grasped by our minds, which have feasted on half-truths for so long.

The important thing is not that we fully understand Jesus, but that we just keep following because, well, where else would we go? It's not the most heroic statement of faith, but if it keeps us tied to Jesus it is good enough.

❦

Jesus' Second Touch

"I can see people, but they look like trees, walking."

Mark 8:24

READ MARK 8:22-26

Jesus had just entered the town of Bethsaida when some people brought a blind man to him. Jesus put saliva on the blind man's eyes, laid hands upon him, and asked, "Can you see anything?" The man's vision had come back, but it was not very clear. It took a second touch from the Savior before the man saw everything clearly.

Why didn't Jesus heal him completely the first time? We don't know. Commentators of the Bible love to speculate about this, but we just don't know for sure. Why hasn't Jesus completely healed you or your loved ones by now? Again, people love to speculate, but we don't really know. It seems that the point of the passage is that eventually we will see clearly, but not right now.

Actually, all of us spend a lot of time between these two ministries by Jesus. When he first gets hold of us we know something is different but the details are still confusing. Only later does the Lord's work in our lives come into sharp focus. Why doesn't he make everything perfect when first we become Christians? We still don't know for sure, but maybe the need for this second touch allows room for our faith to grow. By faith we can at least see that we are in the hands of a Savior. It is enough.

❦

The Faith to Wait

Wait for the Lord; be strong, and let your heart take courage; wait for the Lord!

Psalm 27:14

READ PSALM 27

David was the most powerful king in the history of Israel. So isn't it fascinating that he associated strength and courage with waiting? We would think that a king wouldn't have to wait for much. That's because we assume that the whole point of having strength and courage is to be able to push our way into our dreams. Yet as powerful as he was, King David didn't make any of his dreams come true. Every good thing in his life came as a blessing from the hand of God.

According to the Bible, a blessing is the thing we most want, and it can come only as a gift from God. Furthermore, here's the hard part: whenever someone in the Bible received a blessing, it arrived sooner or later than it was expected. Usually later.

Why do God's blessings arrive late so often? Maybe it is because waiting for a blessing is the best way for our faith to grow strong and courageous. By waiting, our souls are given time to turn away from the thing we most want and to turn back to the God from whom all blessings flow. Then we realize that the real blessing isn't that we may finally get what we have long wanted, but that we are receiving it from the Blesser. Yet by the time you have waited long enough to be that focused on God, you are free from wanting anything or anyone else. Only then are you truly free, which is one of God's greatest blessings.

❦

Weak, But Smart

Be strong in the Lord.

Ephesians 6:10

READ EPHESIANS 6:10-17

With all of the Church's talk about needing a Savior, some people may get the idea that faith is for the weak who can't make it on their own. Well, these people are exactly right. Faith is for the weak. It's also for the smart.

We are all too weak to make it to God without a Savior, and we are even too weak to make it to our own dreams. The smart people are the ones who have found in Jesus Christ all the power of heaven and earth. Of course, that also makes them very strong.

Notice that Paul doesn't say, "Be strong for the Lord." In my dumber moments I keep pretending he did. If you are like me, you are tempted to think that there is a job to be done and the Lord is counting on you. Who are we kidding? One of the great things about being God is that he doesn't need help to get what he wants. No, what Paul told us was to be strong in the Lord.

Things that are strong in something have a lot of it. If you're strong in wealth, you have a lot of money. If you're strong in education, you have learned a lot. If you're strong in determination, you have a lot of drive. The problem with these strong suits is that none of them is strong enough to help you make it either in heaven or on earth. Those who are strong in the Lord, however, have a lot of the Savior in them. Now we are ready to talk about making it to eternal life.

❦

Asking the Right Question

"Who then is this, that even the wind and the sea obey him?"

Mark 4:41

READ MARK 4:35-41

One evening, while the disciples were at sea with Jesus in their boat, a tremendous storm developed. As the boat was being swamped, the disciples asked, "Teacher, do you not care that we are perishing?" In every life there are times when you hit storms. You get a phone call from a doctor who has bad news. Your child tells you that her marriage is breaking up. Your boss enters the office, shuts the door, and starts to talk about downsizing. He's sorry. Dark clouds begin to form. A fierce wind blows. And waves start crashing into the little boat you call life. You pray, "Jesus, don't you care that I am perishing?"

We are told that Jesus then rebuked the wind and told the sea to be still. Then he looked at the disciples and asked, "Why are you afraid? Have you no faith?" Does faith mean that we should not be afraid of the storms of life? Well, yes. By faith we choose to believe that in spite of the storms we are going to be OK, because Jesus is on board and Jesus cares.

After Jesus calmed the storm, the disciples asked him a third question. "Who is this?" It doesn't matter how much time you have spent with Jesus; there is more to him than you know, and there is nothing like going through a storm to help you discover that. Perhaps that is even the purpose of life's dark storms. They help us discover more about living with the Savior.

❦

Seeing and Hearing His Signs

Bring forth the people who are blind, yet have eyes, who are deaf, yet have ears!... You are my witnesses, says the Lord.

Isaiah 43:8,10

READ ISAIAH 43:1-10

Scripture consistently refers to us as a people who have eyes and ears, but who cannot see God or hear his Word. Often that is because we turn our eyes toward our long list of things to do, and our ears toward voices that will flatter us if only we do what they demand. Blinded by our capacity for work, is it any wonder that we stumble through life, asking where God is?

Faith is almost a synonym for vision. It is what allows us to see, to witness, God's presence. Faith is what allows us to survive, even enjoy, today because we've seen that which is not apparent—God is with us. Unless you really do see that, you will be doomed to filling in for God as a poor substitute.

By contrast, those who see that God is active in the world are freed from such a ridiculous challenge. When we hear about Rwanda, Bosnia, the Middle East, or the inner city of Washington, D.C., God isn't asking us to do his work for him. He is asking us to be his distinctive people, namely, to see and hear what the rest of the world cannot—the signs of his involvement. Only then will we know what to do.

The real gift of faith is that if you believe God is at work in the world, you won't have to focus so intensely on fixing it. It is enough to believe and then to do the right thing as an act of faith in God.

❦

A Vision We Can't See

There is still a vision for the appointed time.... If it seems to tarry, wait for it; it will surely come.

Habakkuk 2:3

READ HABAKKUK 2:1-4

Habakkuk was tired of waiting for God. Eventually he climbed up a watchtower and refused to move until he saw an answer to his prayer. I understand that frustration. If we didn't believe God was involved in our lives we could keep our expectations of him pretty low. Yet our faith demands more than that. We do not expect that he will give us everything we want, but God should at least be true to his own promises. For example, the Bible makes it clear that God will lead you into the future with a great vision for your life. So it is reasonable to ask God, "What do you want?"

Those who do not believe in God are not burdened by figuring out what God wants. They simply develop their own visions for life. Yet those of us who have tried that, and repeatedly made big mistakes, are now determined to follow the vision God has for us. The only problem is that sometimes it is hard to see the vision.

Finally, a word from God came to Habakkuk. What he received was not a vision, but rather a promise that a vision would come. Interestingly, that satisfied Habakkuk. My guess is that it would be enough for us as well. We don't really need the details of our future. That can unfold as part of the natural drama of life. What we need is just enough vision to see the God who is leading us there.

❦

Opening Our Hands

Immediately they left their nets and followed him.

Matthew 4:20

READ MATTHEW 4:18-22

I am always amazed at this verse. It describes Peter and Andrew's response when Jesus invited them to become his disciples. Jesus then called to James and John, and again we are told "immediately they left the boat, their father, and followed him." How are we to account for these radical choices? Did all of these men just have a really bad day at work? Were they looking for a way to get out of a dull job? No, there is something more here. They left not only their jobs and families, but even their identities. They were betting everything on Jesus.

To follow Jesus, we all have to leave something behind. Usually it involves our most cherished sources of security. That is because we will never be free to receive the new thing Jesus will give us until our hands have let go of the hopes to which we have been clinging.

Different people cling to different things. Some are clinging to their anger or hurts, others to their great expectations for how life is supposed to turn out. Still others cling to the faith of their childhood and are frightened to ask new questions. Many of us want to see exactly where Jesus is leading us before we leave the places where we would prefer to stay. Yet as the disciples eventually learned, the point of following Jesus is not really to get somewhere special, but simply to follow him. It is Jesus that is placed in our empty hands.

❦

Being in Faith

For by grace you have been saved through faith, and this is not your own doing; it is the gift of God.

Ephesians 2:8

READ EPHESIANS 2:1-10

Christians are used to talking about faith as if it were a possession. We speak of "having faith," or sometimes, "keeping faith," and the last thing we want to do is "lose our faith." Thus, by holding on to faith we assume that we have another tool with which to pursue our goals in life. The Bible, however, rarely speaks of faith as if it were something we own. It is more typical of the Bible to describe faith as something that owns us.

Actually, faith is quite similar to another virtue called love. We usually don't say a person has love for somebody else; rather, we say that someone is in love. The difference is more than semantics. By claiming that we are in love we admit that we have been overwhelmed by a great commitment to another person. Sometimes it hits us at first sight, and at other times it develops slowly, but at no time could we claim to be in perfect control of the love. More honestly, we know that love has the power to control us.

Similarly, faith in God is a wonderful commitment. It may come slowly or in a moment, but once it gets hold of us it changes just about everything. As with love, we don't always know where our faith will lead us. That is what creates the drama in life for most Christians. We may even struggle with our faith, or try to deny that it exists, but in the end most saints will tell you that it is pretty hard to fall out of faith.

❧

Where Faith Is Found

Return to your home and declare how much God has done for you.

Luke 8:39

READ LUKE 8:26-39

Typically when Jesus called disciples to leave home and follow him, they weren't planning on doing anything like that. They had settled lives, with families and businesses to run. In order to follow him they were going to have to leave everything they valued. It was the only way they could discover faith in their Lord. Once they discovered faith, however, they lost their fear. And without fear, these disciples could turn the world upside down.

By contrast, after Jesus healed a man driven crazy by demons in Gerasene, the man begged Jesus to take him with him when he left. Refusing this request, Jesus told the man to stay in the city and simply declare how much God had done for him. This was asking a lot, because the people of Gerasene had banished the man to live in a cemetery while he was crazy with demons. Staying in that town would not be easy for him.

It seems that the guiding principle for Jesus' decisions about who should leave and who should stay is that he always sends us to the place where we are most dependent on a Savior. If your demon is the fear of change, that means you will be hitting the road more than you want. Yet if you are tormented more by the thought of settling into a difficult place, it means you will be staying right where you are. In either case, your hope will come not from where you are, but from whom you find mercy.

♣

The Danger of Making People Happy

*When the people saw that Moses delayed to come down
from the mountain, the people gathered around Aaron, and
said to him, "Come, make gods for us."*

Exodus 32:1

READ EXODUS 32:1-35

Moses had been up on Mount Sinai for a very long time, having an
incredible encounter with God. Yet down below, in the desert, the
people were having anything but a revival. They were worried about
food and water and the fact that they were a very long way from the
Promised Land. Neither God nor his prophet was anywhere to be
seen. So the Hebrews turned to Aaron and asked him to come up with
a new god for them.

Aaron's great failure was not just that he made the gold calf for the
people, but that he never learned how to help them worship the true
God that they did not understand. Instead, he assumed it was his job
to give the people what they wanted, and to take away their anxieties.
Maybe he really cared about them and just wanted them to be happy.

The Aaron school of compassion is alive and well today, but it
works no better for us than it did for him. We can never do enough to
relieve someone's fears. Our mission is not to be the Savior, but to draw
people to their only God, whose hope always seems to be delayed.
Only then are we helping them discover faith. Perhaps the greatest
danger to the faith of those around us is our ability to fix their problems.

❦

A Step of Faith

So when those who bore the ark had come to the Jordan, and the feet of the priests bearing the ark were dipped in the edge of the water, the waters flowing from above stood still.
Joshua 3:15-16

READ JOSHUA 3:1-17

This was the second time the Hebrews had crossed the water. The first time had been forty years before, when God had parted the Red Sea. Now they were about to enter the Promised Land. There were several things about this second water crossing that were noticeably different from the first, but the most significant one is what we have come to call "the step of faith." God expected something to have happened to the people during their time in the wilderness. He no longer considered them to be frightened runaway slaves who had to see divided water before they would pass through. Now he asked them to step into the undivided Jordan water, believing God would be faithful in parting the waters.

Life in the wilderness is not easy, but it does serve a sacred purpose—it is the place where we learn faith. In the desert places of life we wonder how we will survive but discover God is our hope. We often get lost but discover Jesus Christ is our Savior. We are frightened but discover that the Holy Spirit is our comfort. With this vision of God's faithfulness before us, we can then enter into his promised future without knowing how he will provide.

The trick to taking steps of faith is to look at God rather than at the barriers before us.

NINE

A Future Full of Hope

❦

Only After Death

We felt that we had received the sentence of death so that we would rely not on ourselves but on God who raises the dead.
2 Corinthians 1:9

READ 2 CORINTHIANS 1:3-11

Have you ever been in a situation that was completely hopeless? Perhaps it was a job or a relationship or a disease that was beating you down, and there was no reason to think it would improve. You prayed and prayed that God would deliver you from this, but nothing changed. When we find ourselves in these crises, according to the apostle Paul, it feels as though we have "received the sentence of death." It is then that we are tempted to despair.

There is an alternative. Paul claims this is also an opportunity to rely on our God, who has a history of raising people from the dead. What we prefer is for God to step in at the last moment and prevent our deathlike experiences. Yet his preference is often for a resurrection, which can only follow a death. Those who have gone through this claim that the new life they have received is a whole lot better than the one they were afraid of losing, but along the way they were mostly focused on what they were losing.

To be a people of faith does not mean that we don't struggle to prevent loss, or that we cannot grieve when we have lost something cherished. It does mean that we refuse to grieve as those who have no hope. For even if we lose, we win the best gift of all, which is the new life that only God can give us.

179

✿

Soul-Weary

"Go out and stand on the mountain before the Lord, for the Lord is about to pass by."

1 Kings 19:11

READ 1 KINGS 19:1-21

Elijah was burnt out. He was alone, exhausted, discouraged, and running away from his problems. In fact, he fell into such serious despair that he asked God just to kill him. The fascinating thing is that this came right after the greatest victory of his life, when he called fire down out of the sky. Elijah's ministry was a huge success. So why was he so discouraged?

Our darkest moments frequently follow our greatest victories. When we are not just tired, but soul-weary, we are most susceptible to losing our hope. So God led the prophet to Mount Horeb to give him his own spiritual revival. A powerful rock-splitting wind came by, "but the Lord was not in the wind." Then an earthquake and fire, but the Lord was not in them either. These were symbols of high drama to which Elijah was accustomed. Yet God came to him in the "sound of sheer silence."

If you are like me, you are not a fan of silence. We live noisy lives, and much of the noise is of our own making as we try so hard all week to pull a little fire out of the sky. That is why God created the Sabbath. The literal meaning of Sabbath is to stop it. Cut it out. Be quiet. The more dramatic your work becomes, the more you will need silence. The wind and fire may be exciting, but the soul has to have quiet to hear the still, small voice of God's hope.

❦

Only One World

God did not send the Son into the world to condemn the world,
but in order that the world might be saved through him.

John 3:17

READ JOHN 3:16-21

Paul Tournier has claimed that the world is like a great ship that is disabled. In the beginning, the crew disobeyed the captain's orders and handled the ship badly. Since then, sometimes by noble ideals and sometimes out of self-preservation, successive crews have feverishly tried to repair the damage. Yet their fear and desperation have created such panic that the ship has been handled worse than ever. The sailors argue so vehemently among themselves that it is impossible to hear the captain's orders. Thus, the ship never escapes the storms. Everyone on board claims to be a victim of the deadly chain of events that began long ago. Yet each is also at fault, and contributes, even with good intentions, to the confusion.

There is only one world. We are all vulnerable if there is a crisis anywhere on the ship. We dare not assume that the pathos of the poor or the problems of ecology, population, or violence do not affect us. Yet before we jump into the fray of competing rescue strategies, we must remember that this world has a God.

If hope is to be found—and I believe it is—we have to have courage in these times. Not the courage to rush into the panic with more argument and blame, but the greater courage to be quiet long enough to listen to the captain's orders. We call that worship.

What we will then discover is that not only are we all in the same boat, but so is the captain. He never abandons ship.

❦

Resurrecting Hope

This man went to Pilate and asked for the body of Jesus.

Luke 23:52

Read Luke 23:50-56

Joseph of Arimathea is introduced to us as a good and righteous man, who was waiting expectantly for the kingdom of God. Luke also tells us that he was a member of the ruling council, but disagreed with its plan to have Jesus killed. Maybe that was because Joseph saw what Jesus had done, or heard his teaching, and believed that he was the One to bring about the kingdom of God. Maybe.

All we know for sure is that after Jesus was dead, Joseph was the one to pull him off the cross and place him in a tomb. It must have cost Joseph a lot to do this. Not only were these rock-hewn tombs incredibly expensive, but he was clearly going to have to pay an even higher cost when his colleagues on the council heard about his tender care for Jesus. Yet if you asked Joseph, he would have said the greatest cost was that he was burying his hope.

Joseph was more devoted to the dead Savior than many of us are to the risen one. When we do not get what we want from Jesus, when we want it, we quickly abandon him and turn to more promising saviors. Yet Joseph invites us to stay with Jesus even after our devotion appears hopeless. Go ahead and bury him if you have to. Admit that you feel hopeless. Yet stay by the tomb and do not turn to other hopes, because the story isn't over yet. Joseph was going to get to use that tomb for someone else.

❦

Leaving Comfortable Despair

"Where, O death, is your victory? Where, O death, is your sting?"

1 Corinthians 15:55

READ 1 CORINTHIANS 15:50-58

I've never met anyone who didn't believe in death. That's because we have seen too much of it. We've buried too many loved ones, too many relationships and dreams, to deny that death is real. It's the resurrection that is hard to believe.

Paul tells us that after Easter, that is exactly backward. It is the resurrection that is real, and death that we ought to be doubting. Jesus did not come back from the dead just to regain his own life, but to defeat the power of death and despair over all of us. So despair is really a sin. It is claiming to have more faith in death than in Jesus.

In the year 387, an old preacher named John Chrysostom climbed into his pulpit in Antioch on Easter Sunday. It had been a hard year for the city. Rome had conscripted most of the men into the army to fight distant wars in the north while women and children remained behind to scavenge for food. The people despaired that their lives would ever get better. Chrysostom boldly told his congregation, "Your resignation assumes God is dead. Do not be so certain. He who embraced death has defeated its power over us. He who went down to hell liberated every city held captive by hell's despair. Christ is risen! Open the doors of your comfortable despair, that the great storms of hope may blow life into us again."

What about you? Isn't it time for you also to leave your comfortable despair?

❦

Settling Into Today's Life

*For surely I know the plans I have for you, says the Lord,
plans for your welfare and not for harm, to give you a future
filled with hope.*

Jeremiah 29:11

READ JEREMIAH 29:1-14

This verse has been an inspiration to people of faith for a long time. We have a copy of it hanging on a wall in our home. I love the hope and reassurance it provides. Yet it is important to remember its context.

The words were first spoken to the Hebrews who were exiled in Babylon. They had been dragged there by their enemy Nebuchadnezzar after he leveled the city of Jerusalem and destroyed everything they held dear. The Hebrews were not where they wanted to be in life, and they were bitterly angry at the people who held them captive. That is why the rest of the prophecy is so striking. Since the future belonged to the Lord, the people were told to settle into the life that they now had. They were instructed to "build houses and live in them, plant gardens ... take wives and have sons and daughters." Then came the real surprise: "Seek the welfare of the city where I have sent you into exile and pray to the Lord on its behalf."

If we really believe that the end of the story is "filled with hope," we are free from anxiety about today. In fact, our hearts should be so overflowing with gratitude that we are even able to care for the people who have hurt us. So the point of Jeremiah's prophecy is not that we should just hang on until things improve. His point is to give us joy in the opportunities of today.

❦

Not in the Nick of Time

Though Jesus loved Martha and her sister and Lazarus, after having heard that Lazarus was ill, he stayed two days longer in the place where he was.

John 11:5

READ JOHN 11:1-44

We may not think of Jesus as being the kind of person who had personal friends. We know about the disciples and the multitudes that flocked around him, but we assume that Jesus was too busy for things like friendships. According to John's Gospel, however, Jesus was very close to Lazarus and his sisters and was a frequent guest at their home.

One day when Jesus was out of town he received word that his friend was very ill. We would expect that since Jesus was easily interrupted by strangers who needed healing, surely he would rush back to take care of his beloved friend. Yet Jesus didn't hurry. And Lazarus died.

Later it becomes apparent that Jesus was determined to raise Lazarus from the dead. Yet still we wonder, "Why didn't Jesus just prevent this death?" There are several answers to this question in the text. He wanted the disciples to develop greater faith. He wanted his friends to realize he was more than a repairman. He wanted the people to discover that he was "the resurrection and the life." He wanted you and me to discover that salvation usually comes not just in the nick of time, but after it is too late. It is then that this Savior can raise our hopes from the dead. The reason he doesn't hurry is because he loves us too much to let our anxieties become our god.

❦

With You at Dark and Dawn

You have kept count of my tossings; put my tears in your bottle.

Psalm 56:8

Read Psalm 56

Do you ever go to bed thinking about something so painful that you just can't get to sleep? You toss and turn for a while; you stare at the ceiling; you watch the numbers on the alarm clock. Yet all the while you're thinking, worrying, regretting, or maybe even nurturing your anger.

Maybe something awful happened that day and you just can't let go of it. Maybe you are worried about what is about to happen. Or maybe one night you are simply overwhelmed by the realization that your life is not working out as you had dreamed. Your heart feels like it is about to break in half from holding so much sorrow.

The late-night tears are the worst kind. They make us feel so lonely. No one sees them. No one is there to comfort or reassure. No one, except God, who, according to David, counts and saves every tear in a bottle.

Why does God save our tears? I really don't know, but it is comforting to realize that he has not forgotten about our dark nights of restless sorrow. And because he is there in the darkest moments of life, we know that he will be there when the sun finally rises and the new day begins. Once we have come to believe this, we can end our long nights the way David ends this psalm, confident that we can now "walk before God in the light of life."

❧

Keeping Your Eyes Open

"They have taken away my Lord, and I do not know where they have laid him."

John 20:13

READ JOHN 20:1-18

Remember that Easter is never what we had in mind. Scripture portrays it as an unexpected, shocking surprise. The story we would have written would never have included a resurrection, because we would not have allowed Jesus to make it as far as the cross. Like the early disciples, we have expectations of Jesus—things we need him to do. Yet when he goes to the cross on Good Friday, he will take all of our hopes with him.

Life is so very fragile. Sooner or later loss will invade every neatly ordered life. Some will lose their marriages, others their health, and still others will lose success and the dreams of their youth. As we watch these things slip by, we may pray that Jesus will fix things. Yet after the cross, there is no guarantee.

However (the gospel always turns on a great "however"), what is promised is that when we go to the tomb to grieve, we will find it empty. The great surprise of Easter is that loss is not the end of the story. It's an unavoidable part of the story, but it's not the last chapter. The last chapter is always devoted to the new creation of God.

It's fascinating that Mary Magdalene was so focused on missing Jesus that she didn't recognize he was the gardener, until he called her name. I believe that from that day on, she kept her eyes open. In fact, she probably looked for Jesus in everyone she met.

❦

Another Dark Night in Bethlehem

"Do not be afraid; for see—I am bringing you good news of great joy for all the people."

Luke 2:10

READ LUKE 2:8-14

I am amazed at how much fear was associated with the birth of Jesus. The angels kept announcing that they had great news from God, and everyone's response was to be filled with fear. It is striking that the arrival of the Savior brings our anxieties to the surface.

Before we can approach the Christ Child, we first must tell the truth about our own fears. For it is not in outrunning our fears that we find hope. That just makes us compulsive and driven. Our fears can chase us like a demon through our whole lives. Yet if we stop running long enough to confront the soul's dark fear, then what once appeared demonic can actually become angelic.

Our fears are the angels that bring God to us. It is always as we approach the thing we most dread that we find the light of hope, and his name is Emmanuel, the God with us.

It was just another dark night in Bethlehem. Suddenly, the skies were ripped open by the glory of God. An angel proclaimed, "Do not be afraid, for I bring you good news of great joy for all the people. For to you is born this day a Savior."

❦

An Open Future

And suddenly there was a great earthquake; for an angel of the Lord, descending from heaven, came and rolled back the stone and sat on it.... For fear of him the guards shook and became like dead men.

Matthew 28:2-4

READ MATTHEW 28:1-10

You don't understand Easter if it doesn't scare you. This is not a sentimental spring holiday that glibly reassures us everything will turn out as we had planned. Easter has very little to do with our plans. It has everything to do with the unpredictable work of our Savior. Not even death could keep Jesus from bringing us back to God. That, of course, is the hope that the church has to offer the world. Yet a world with hope is not a very predictable place. Anything can happen.

Prior to Easter, our plans for life were essentially to gather up as many good days as possible before we returned to the grave. The problem with that plan, though, was that it wasn't life. It was just the postponement of death. Since Easter, death has been removed as the ending of our story. Now it is just another chapter, and it is certainly not the last one. This means our future is open-ended. According to Genesis, that was how we were created to live from the beginning. Now God alone can create our lives.

If our future is open, then nothing is certain along the way to that future. Well, almost nothing. We can, at least, count on Jesus Christ continuing his work of salvation. Once we discover that he is missing from the grave, there is no telling where he will again appear in his search to give life to those who are living as if they are already dead.

✤

Squeezing Through

"Strive to enter through the narrow door."

Luke 13:24

Read Luke 13:22-30

Those who applied for the job of being a disciple often worried Jesus. The learning curve was sky high. The hours were terrible. The pay was minimal. One's colleagues in this line of work could drive one batty. The boss, well, the boss was very unpredictable. And promotions took a lifetime. Following Jesus was hard work.

We live in a society where the constant goal is to make life easier. We have timesaving devices in our kitchens, our offices, and even our cars. So how strange it is to hear Jesus warning that following him involves a lot of striving. If he isn't going to make our lives easier, why bother? Because he alone can lead us to salvation. Yet getting to that salvation is like struggling to squeeze through a narrow, little door.

In fact, the door is so narrow that we can't hold onto anything and still make it through. Not our trophies and achievements. Not our relationships. Not even our dreams. We have to drop them all if we're going to fit through the door called salvation. Yet that is just one of the ways Jesus leads us to hope. None of those things we are holding will save us. Only Jesus, and we have to come to him empty-handed.

On the other side of the narrow door, you'll discover that Jesus is waiting for you, holding all the things you cherish. They weren't your salvation. They were your blessings. And you'll never be able to enjoy them until you stop counting on them to be your savior.

۴

Eternal Embrace

"Blessed are the dead who from now on die in the Lord."
Revelation 14:13

READ REVELATION 14:13

Recently, Henri Nouwen died. He was a Roman Catholic priest and one of the Church's great teachers on spirituality. His writings have had a profound influence on my understanding of the Christian life. I will greatly miss the joy of rushing to the bookstore to grab his newest book, and being so excited that I have to start reading it at the stoplights on the way home. He spoke at my seminary graduation, and I will never forget his challenge to just nurture our own love for Jesus. If we are certain of that, he said, we can handle all of the confusion and ambiguity that will cloud our ministry to real people.

It is striking that Nouwen concluded one of his last books, *Living as the Beloved*, with a reference to his thoughts about death. They serve as his final words to the Church: "Am I afraid to die? I am every time I let myself be seduced by the noisy voices of my world telling me that my 'little life' is all I have and advising me to cling to it with all my might. But when I let these voices move to the background of my life and listen to that small soft voice calling me to the Beloved, I know there is nothing to fear and that dying is the greatest act of love, the act that leads me into the eternal embrace of my God whose love is everlasting." Heaven's gain is our loss, for now.

❦

Shedding Our Illusions

Mary said to the angel, "How can this be, since I am a virgin?"
Luke 1:34

READ LUKE 1:26-38

It is important to remember that God's entry into the world came in the form of an unanticipated pregnancy, which shattered the respectable, reasonable dreams of Mary and Joseph. Our experience of God's arrival may be the same.

The difficulty of the virgin birth was never meant to be a theological or scientific difficulty. According to the text, it was meant to be a personal difficulty, a difficulty of receiving something we had not planned on receiving—a visit from God. This element of surprise, even unwanted surprise, is critical to understanding the relevance of the Christmas story.

The sudden arrival of the Holy Spirit into our lives is never what we had in mind. What we had in mind was a source of hope that was a little less painful, and something that involved a whole lot more control. We didn't plan on loss, or embarrassment. However, neither did we plan on the valued gifts and relationships we have in life.

Before we can really hear the Good News of "unto you is born this day a Savior who is Christ the Lord," we first have to face the hard news of our need for salvation. There is nothing for which we need salvation more than the illusion that we can get exactly what we have in mind for life. The Christmas message is that the Holy Spirit of God has conceived something in our lives. Maybe we have thought it would be our ruin. In fact, it is the only hope we've got.

❦

Waiting in the Dark

My soul waits for the Lord, more than watchmen for the morning.

Psalm 130:6, RSV

READ PSALM 130

While I was in college I worked as a night security guard. My job was to make sure no one stole anything from a completely empty office building. It wasn't a very challenging job, but it gave me a lot of time to do schoolwork, since I was alone for the whole night. From ten until midnight I was very productive. During the next few hours both the quality and the quantity of my work tapered off. By four o'clock I was doing everything I could to stay awake, which excluded any more homework. The last couple of hours were always the hardest. I didn't think about anything but the sunrise, when I could finally go home.

You also know what it is like to be a watchman, waiting for morning. We all have to spend time in the darkness that is caused by the grief, heartache, and disappointments of life. Early on, we try to throw ourselves into work, but that only helps for a while. We would love to reach out to others, but when it feels dark in our souls we are always alone. We try to think about our options, but they are too hard to see in the dark. Eventually we just succumb to waiting for the sun to rise.

Actually, that is the most hopeful thing we can do. Only when we are exhausted do we remember it is for the Lord that we are waiting. Only he can bring enough light back into our lives that, at last, we can find our way home again.

TEN

Jesus: In the Presence of the Savior

❦

Letting Go of Jesus

Jesus said to her, "Do not hold on to me ..."

John 20:17

READ JOHN 20:11-18

When Mary Magdalene discovered that Jesus was risen from the dead she called him "teacher" and reached out to embrace him. Then Jesus said a very strange thing: "Don't hold on to me." This is not my favorite part of the Easter story. If I were writing this scene, I would have a big tearful embrace followed by Jesus saying, "Go get the others and tell them I'm back. We're going home to settle down." My guess is that was what Mary would have preferred as well. Yet Jesus didn't say that. He said, "Don't hold on to me."

The Christian life is a never-ending process of losing the Jesus we were holding only to discover a more unmanageable form of him. Mary thought she had captured him in a safe expectation by making him her teacher, but in reality that was just another tomb. And Jesus won't stay in a tomb.

Our image of Jesus is reflective of what we need hope to look like. Yet there comes a time when that image needs to die because there is more to Jesus than we know. At Easter we encounter a risen Savior who has a new vision for our future. After the resurrection things do not return to normal. That's the good news. It's basic to everything else the New Testament teaches. After Jesus has defeated death, nothing can be seen as predictable. There is no normal. There is no ordinary. Not when a Savior is loose.

❦

The Land of the Bland

I pray that you may have the power to comprehend, with all the saints, what is the breadth and length and height and depth, and to know the love of Christ.

Ephesians 3:18-19

Read Ephesians 3:14-21

Most Christians I know could use a lot more passion in their lives. We do not cry nearly enough, or laugh loudly enough. I doubt that is because we don't want the drama. I think it is because we are scared of it. We have been taught to live too much of life on the flat plane in the middle, between the highs and lows, where we settle for reasonable expectations that starve the passion out of life.

Jesus spent a whole lot of time at the high and low ends. That is because as God in the flesh, Jesus lived with a passionate dream. It wasn't very realistic considering the options, but he consistently peered beyond the reasonable possibilities to call people to a very dramatic life with God. When he saw a shriveled little tax collector do the impossible thing of giving half his money back to the poor, Jesus became so elated that he threw a party at Zacchaeus' house. When he saw the temple defiled by those who had no regard for holiness, Jesus went crazy with anger and turned the place upside down. It was so like him to become furious when he saw humanity conduct business as usual, as if there was no sacred. Yet that is exactly what we do when we insist on a cautious life.

God will not be contained by any of our expectations, least of all those that attempt to domesticate his terrifying creativity. Beneath the thin veneer of our decent and orderly routines there is probably more drama than we want to see.

❧

Into the Depths

I dwell in the high and holy place, and also with those who are contrite and humble in spirit.

Isaiah 57:15

READ ISAIAH 57:14-19

To dwell with the sacred God of creation is the greatest joy of life. It is also the hardest thing we do. To say that God is sacred means that he does not explain himself to us. It means he is too mysterious to fit our plans for self-improvement. It means that God is not our best friend, our secret lover, or our good luck charm. It even means that it is just as frightening as it is delightful to stand in his presence.

Our created relationship with God is one in which we are, at the same time, both irresistibly drawn to him and yet also humbled by the grandeur of his holiness. The sacred can never be contained by our fervent prayers, our theological boxes, or our great need to have God on our side. For this reason, we often turn to other gods that are more manageable. Some search for the sacred in work, or in relationships, or in some vague nonbiblical spirituality. Yet these substitute gods do not satisfy us. That is because we have been created with a craving for the sacred. Nothing else will do.

The best news about our God, though, is that he will not stay in the high and holy place. In Jesus Christ, God has come looking for us, because he loves us. And since the cross, there is no limit to the depths this sacred God will sink in finding us.

❦

Breaking the World's Power

"Take courage; I have conquered the world!"

John 16:33

READ JOHN 16:25-33

When Jesus said these words, he looked like anything but a world conqueror. The crowd that praised his arrival into Jerusalem had abandoned him. He had just completed his last supper with the twelve disciples. Even as he spoke, Judas was betraying him. In fact, he was moments away from being arrested, tried, and hung on a cross between two criminals. Frankly, it looked like the world was about to conquer Jesus.

Of course, Jesus predicted all of these events. More importantly, he also predicted that he would rise from the dead. The disciples had heard Jesus talk about his resurrection, but they couldn't quite figure that out. Yet, as Jesus went to the cross, they were very clear about his losing power, respectability, and even his life. Most of the time the same thing is true for us. We have a much clearer concept of what we are losing than of what the resurrection means for us. Most of the time we don't feel like conquerors in life.

In his resurrection, though, Jesus defeated death. Anyone who can do that has just broken the back of the world's power. Until Easter, death was the one thing of which we were certain. It was the world's final trump card over life. Now that we have a Savior who conquers even death, clearly Jesus can save us from anything. I think this means that of all the emotions we may have in life, fear is probably the one that Christians can use the least. After death has been defeated, what in the world are you afraid of?

❦

Everything in Christ

Blessed be the God and Father of our Lord Jesus Christ, who has blessed us in Christ with every spiritual blessing in the heavenly places.

Ephesians 1:3

READ EPHESIANS 1:3-10

Most of us don't feel that we have already received every blessing heaven has to offer. Yet according to the apostle Paul, we certainly have. When God gave us his Son, he gave us everything. There is nothing left in heaven. This means that we have to be very careful about asking for more. How could we ask for more than Jesus Christ?

Are you looking for more love? Look instead at the love you have already received in Christ. He was so passionate about you that he was literally dying to love you. Until you have learned to receive his love, you will never be satisfied with the love of anyone else, because you will constantly be expecting him or her to be your savior.

Are you looking for more health? In Christ, you were given eternal life. This doesn't mean that Jesus is unconcerned about the diseases of life, but his healing of your body is never more than a sign of the work that he has already accomplished in healing your soul.

Are you looking for more direction? All the earth is already his, so Christ isn't nearly so concerned about where you go, or what you do, as he is about who you are. The only direction that really matters is the one that returns you to the place where you are grateful for having received more than you can see.

❦

Beyond Belief

Not everyone who says to me Lord, Lord, shall enter the kingdom of heaven but he who does the will of my father who is in heaven.

Matthew 7:21, RSV

Read Matthew 7:21-23

If this were all Jesus had said, it would provide what we expected from him. We expect him to say that it is not enough to call ourselves followers of Christ. The real issue is what we are doing. Yet as we read on in the text we discover that Jesus also rejects those who are doing some pretty impressive things: "Many will say to me, 'Lord, Lord, did we not prophesy in your name, and cast out demons in your name, and do many deeds of power in your name?' And I will declare to them, 'I never knew you; go away from me, you evildoers.'"

If it isn't what we say, and it isn't what we do, then what is the criterion for entering the kingdom? Apparently, the people who enter the kingdom are those whom Jesus knows.

Living as a Christian is not a matter of what you do or say, but of what God has done. In Jesus, he has come to know you. The Pharisees knew tons of theology and they did all they could to be righteous, but they rejected Jesus because he claimed to embody God's gift of a relationship. It is possible to hide behind our religion as a way of avoiding a personal encounter with God, who wants most of all just to know us. Never settle for just knowing about God, when it is possible actually to know God.

❦

Beyond the Cross

Since, then, we have a great high priest who has passed through the heavens, Jesus, the Son of God, let us hold fast to our confession.

Hebrews 4:14

READ HEBREWS 4:14-16

One of the greatest mistakes we can make about Jesus is to limit his work to dying on the cross. He was once a sacrificial lamb; he is now a Great High Priest.

When we think only about the cross, we reduce Jesus to a historical figure, and we reduce salvation to little more than a second chance. "He paid for your sins with his life, back there, two thousand years ago," we sometimes say. "He gave you another chance, so don't mess up again." This admonishment creates enormous pressure on us to live a life worthy of Jesus' incredible sacrifice. Yet it doesn't matter how hard we try to demonstrate our gratitude, or how many chances we get, we are still going to sin. That's because we're addicted to sin.

This is why the gospel story doesn't stop with Good Friday. After rising from the dead, the Son of God ascended into heaven, where he sits at the right hand of the Father. From there he intercedes on our behalf, as a Priest who appropriates the sacrifice of his life in the past for the sins of our life today. That doesn't just mean that Jesus has our tab covered. It also means that, like a great priest, he is "not unable to sympathize with our weaknesses," but tenderly leads us deeper into the life-changing grace of his Father. Always remember: Jesus is not done with you.

❦

First Believe

"But who do you say that I am?"

Matthew 16:15

READ MATTHEW 16:13-29

Jesus and Peter had been working on this question for some time. It was behind all of the miracles, parables, and teaching. Yet now the time had come to confront the question head-on. Who do you say that I am? At first, Peter dodged the issue by giving answers he had heard from others. "Some say John the Baptist, but others Elijah, and still others Jeremiah, or one of the prophets." Jesus wouldn't let him off the hook so easily. (Not to mention that those are all wrong answers.) But who do you say that I am?

We face that question every day. It lies behind all of the other questions we encounter, just as it did for Peter. Someone asks us to do something that is wrong. Our response is essentially a way of deciding if Jesus is our Lord. We have to accept change we would rather not face. We will make it only if we decide that Jesus is our Savior. We find ourselves in a relationship that appears hopeless. The only way to avoid despair is to first believe Jesus is the Son of the Living God, for whom all things are possible.

You've probably hung around churches long enough to know that these are the right answers to Jesus' question. Yet the right answers won't help a whole lot when you face the dilemmas of life. Then what you need are convictions that spring from the heart. There is only one way to get them. Answer the question. The chances are good that tomorrow you will have to answer it again.

❦

Serving Someone Else's Son

"You will go before the Lord, to prepare his ways."

Luke 1:76

READ LUKE 1:67-80

When John the Baptist was born, his father, Zechariah, was so happy that he broke out in song. Like many of our hymns, the Song of Zechariah contains four stanzas. The first one is about Jesus. So is the second one. The third one mentions Zechariah's own son, John. Yet the fourth stanza goes back to praising Jesus. So the pattern here is Jesus, Jesus, John, Jesus.

I have visited a lot of fathers of newborn children. I have never heard anyone say, "Yeah, he's a good kid, and someday he's going to grow up to serve someone else's son." No, if a father is going to burst out in song in the delivery room, he's usually singing about his own kid. Eventually, however, this joy turns into expectation, and expectation turns into disappointment. Yet old Zechariah knew that his son was only the third stanza of the hymn. This meant that John grew up knowing he wasn't anybody's savior.

The gospel is not about our dreams. It is about the dreams of Jesus. Our job is just to prepare the way for him. Frankly, we do that best when we are clear about our limitations.

❦

Blinded by the Light

"Saul, Saul, why do you persecute me?"

Acts 9:4

READ ACTS 9:1-9

It is important to remember that Paul was very religious before Jesus got hold of him. Saul, as he was called prior to his conversion, was deeply devoted to God. He was a member of the Pharisees, which was the highly respected conservative party within Judaism. He knew the Scriptures and the great traditions. He was a regular attendee at worship. All of that religious activity was born out of his fervent faith in God. In fact, he was so fervent that he dedicated his time and energy to fighting heresy. The people who bothered Saul the most were the followers of Jesus of Nazareth. One day, while trying to resist these followers, Saul was interrupted by the risen Jesus Christ. The devout Pharisee had been wrong. Very wrong.

It is terrifying for us good religious folks to discover that there is more to God than we know. This isn't a new perspective that we can easily assimilate. To discover a new vision of God is so overwhelming it leaves us with a whole new identity. It is like, well, like being born all over again. We might as well change our name. Everything is different about us.

The fascinating thing about this is that the new life didn't come from all of Paul's theology or his faithfulness to the tradition he inherited. It came only from receiving a vision of Jesus. This doesn't mean that tradition is unimportant. Yet it does mean that until we know Jesus we will never enjoy the new life to which our tradition has been pointing.

❦

The Rescue Mission of Jesus

"Bring in the poor, the crippled, the blind, and the lame."
Luke 14:21

READ LUKE 14:15-24

When I was attending graduate school in Chicago, I would occasionally walk past an inner-city rescue ministry called The Pacific Garden Mission. It had a tacky orange neon cross on the outside that I always found embarrassing. One day as I walked down that street I saw a beautiful new sign with the message, "Welcome to the Art of Living." At first I thought that the rescue mission must be under new management. Yet when I got closer, I could see that the sign belonged to the new condominiums that had been built nearby. Smaller print on the sign promised that these condos would provide "luxury, security, and the chance to meet exciting new people." Suddenly, the old neon cross over the rescue mission looked pretty good to me.

These very different signs describe very different philosophies to "the art of living." The pretty new one assures us that it has to do with moving into the right place, where you will be surrounded by the right kind of people and protected from the wrong kind. The other sign, the embarrassing one, claims that the art of living is to join those under the cross who are in need of being rescued.

To enter the kingdom of God is to walk into the rescue mission of Jesus. There isn't much luxury inside, but there is eternal security, and the opportunity to meet exciting new people. Of course, some of them are poor and homeless, but the art of spiritual living is to see these folks as your neighbors.

❦

Salvation Comes to Call

"Those who drink of the water that I will give them will never be thirsty again."

John 4:14

Read John 4:4–42

One day when Jesus was at a well, he met a woman who had been through five marriages. Now she was living with another man. Apparently, the other women of the village wouldn't associate with her, because, contrary to custom, she came alone to the well in the heat of the day. So this thirsty woman was all alone.

Nothing can hurt us quite like our responses to the thirst of a parched soul. This woman's life illustrates the depths of desperation and loneliness to which a wild pursuit of satisfaction can lead us. It is because she is so thirsty, though, that she finds the Savior. He is the one for whom she has really been longing her whole life. She is so excited about this discovery that she eventually brings the whole town to meet Jesus.

If you have not made so big a mess of life as this woman did, that may reflect only your shallow thirsts. Most of us are leading respectable lives and have not been shamed for our sins. We pay our bills, keep our marriages to a minimum, and hold down good jobs. People would be proud to be seen in public with us. Yet, this allows us to kid ourselves that we are doing just fine without a Savior.

Had it not been for this disgraced woman, whose thirst was too great to settle for respectability, everyone in her village would have missed salvation when it came for a visit.

✿

A Joy That Never Ends

Jesus did this, the first of his signs, in Cana of Galilee, and revealed his glory; and his disciples believed in him.

John 2:11

READ JOHN 2:1-11

I have always been fascinated by Jesus' miracle of turning water into wine at the wedding in Cana of Galilee. The disciples had just abandoned everything to follow him because, in the words of Nathaniel, "You are the king of Israel!" Now, maybe the problem is that I spend too much time inside the beltway, but I expected that the first place the new king would head would be Jerusalem. No, he revealed his glory at a country wedding for a bride who was so insignificant that we never even get her name.

At first, it seemed to be a wasted miracle. No one was healed, fed, or brought back to life. Instead, a lot of people who had already been drinking were just given another 180 gallons of wine. Yet the text is very clear about this—that is how Jesus revealed his glory, and that is why the disciples believed in him. Maybe that is the point. You see, the disciples were also small-town, country people. They knew that this wedding was the bride's one shot at a little happiness in her otherwise harsh life. What Jesus did was demonstrate that he can turn our precious few moments of happiness into a joy that never ends. Once the disciples believed that, they could take on all the power of Jerusalem. Until we discover that Jesus is our Joy, we are going to be of little use to him or to anyone else in this world who is still settling for moments of happiness.

❦

Making Room for a Savior

"No good tree bears bad fruit, nor again does a bad tree bear good fruit."

Luke 6:43

READ LUKE 6:43-45

In the course of a day we receive hundreds of invitations to improve ourselves. Advertisements tell us that if we buy their products we'll become beautiful. Supervisors tell us that if we try harder we'll be successful. Even the people who love us sometimes tell us that if we make a few improvements we will be loved even more. It is easy to get tired of all this help. No one wants to think he or she is simply a construction project in need of renovations. So in frustration we sometimes want to scream out, "I'm fine just the way I am!"

Jesus wouldn't put it exactly like that. He never told people they were fine just the way they were, because that's not true. Yet he didn't offer suggestions for self-improvement, either. It just wouldn't help any more than that dusty old exercise bike you have in the basement. Trying to change yourself by focusing on the externals is like trying to get a bad tree to produce good fruit. You're going to have to get to the root of the problem, and then change from the inside out. And for that you need a Savior. Only in Christ can you become who you really are.

So we don't really need to worry about self-improvement. Instead, we need to worry a great deal about confessing that we really can't fix too much in this world, least of all ourselves. That makes room for Jesus the Savior, and whenever Jesus appears in our lives, well, that's already an improvement.

❦

Along the Way

As they went, they were made clean.

Luke 17:14

READ LUKE 17:11-19

One day Jesus was approached by ten lepers. We aren't told a thing about their families, homes, jobs, or histories. That's what leprosy does. It takes away the appearances that distinguish us. We don't even know their names. They were just "ten lepers."

Most of us have a little leprosy in our lives. Maybe it started as an old hurt, or a lost dream, or a little fear. These things grow over time. If we don't get rid of them, eventually they take over our hearts and then we, too, are known only by our disease. This is just one of the reasons why we need a Savior so desperately.

Jesus told the lepers to show themselves to the priests. That was what people did after they were healed. Yet the diseased lepers weren't healed until they started walking toward the priests. Sometimes Jesus changes us in a miraculous moment. Most of the time, though, he tells us to start moving toward health. He tells us to do the hard work of forgiving, trusting, praying, repairing relationships, and trying again. Along the way, our hearts are healed.

All the lepers were healed, but only one returned to give thanks to Jesus, so apparently our lack of gratitude does not prevent us from receiving mercy. Yet it does prevent us from receiving Jesus. According to this story, the point is not to be healed. The point is to get back to Jesus, and the mark of being with Jesus is not our recovery but our gratitude.

🍂

The Savior We Don't Understand

When they looked up, they saw no one except Jesus himself alone.

Matthew 17:8

READ MATTHEW 17:1-8

When Jesus asked the disciples, "Who do you say that I am?" it was Peter who knew the right answer. "You are the Christ. The Son of the Living God." Yet moments later, when Jesus began to talk about going to a cross, Peter said, "God forbid."

Of all the disciples, it's easiest for me to relate to Peter. He had committed himself to following Jesus. When called upon, he could usually come up with the right answer. And he loved Jesus. Yet he didn't always understand him, especially the part about going to the cross.

So when Jesus invited Peter to climb a mountain with him, it was a troubled disciple who followed. That is the portrait of most followers of Jesus: confused about where Jesus is leading us, disappointed that his dreams always include a cross. On the mountain Peter heard a voice from heaven saying, "This is my Son, the Beloved; with him I am well pleased; listen to him." This terrified Peter so much that he fell on his face. It wasn't the voice that scared him so much as the message. If Peter had to listen to Jesus then he had to accept the cross.

We are told that when Peter lifted his eyes, he saw only Jesus. Not the right answers, the fears, or even the cross. Just the Savior he didn't understand. Yet then Peter knew he would be OK, precisely because he did not understand. That's how salvation works. Nothing you understand is ever going to save you.

❦

Opening Your Heart

The Lord opened her heart.

Acts 16:14

READ ACTS 16:11-15

When Paul and Silas entered the city of Philippi, they met a business-woman named Lydia. She was a dealer of purple cloth. In her society, purple cloth was extremely valuable, worn only by the wealthy. To be a dealer of it meant that she owned something like an ancient Giorgio Armani store. In spite of her considerable success, though, it is striking that Paul and Silas met her at a place of prayer. Clearly she was searching for something more to her life than success. When Paul explained that God had also been searching for her and had come in Jesus Christ to find her, we are told that the Lord opened Lydia's heart. This implies that her heart was closed.

Anyone who is successful can understand why Lydia would have closed her heart. You have to be tough to survive the competition, the office politics, the demanding public, the constant criticism. It doesn't take long to realize that if you keep your heart open at work, it's going to get broken. So, you close it down, and settle for a life with familiar strangers.

Yet once you close your heart, you can't get it open again. It stays closed when you go home, go to church, or return to the places where you are supposed to be safe. It takes a Savior to get your heart open again. Until you let Jesus open your heart to God, you will never be able to open it to anyone else. That also means that if you cannot love someone as much as you want, you first have to return to Jesus.

❦

You Can Stop Pretending

The one who began a good work in you will bring it to completion at the day of Jesus Christ.

Philippians 1:6, RSV

Read Philippians 1:3-11

Most of the self-help market today is not really about helping people. It is about changing them. It is about improving on them until they become somebody else. This market is fed by the great dissatisfaction people have with their lives, and their fears that they are stuck with themselves until they die. Sometimes people come to church hoping that God will do what all the books, seminars, and exercise have failed to do—change them. Yet churches don't talk too much about change. They talk about conversion.

When God converts us, he does not give us a new identity; rather, he allows us to discover what our true identity has been all along. As we open ourselves to the new life that God is creating within us, we discover that this new life does not look totally strange to us. What it looks like is a purer form of ourselves. It is the self we were created to be from the beginning. It is the restoration of the image of God in our lives.

We certainly do not create our own lives. God alone is our Creator. So why then would we think that his work of conversion in our lives would be to something different from what he had intended for us all along? It isn't. The saving work of Jesus Christ is that he finds us after we lose our way in trying to become something other than who we are. That salvation invites us to live the rest of our lives in humble gratitude for the really good life Jesus keeps giving back to us.

❦

Being Faithful in the Mystery

They were terrified as they entered the cloud.

Luke 9:34

READ LUKE 9:28-36

One day Peter, James, and John climbed up a mountain to pray with Jesus. While they were praying, Jesus was transformed. His face changed, his clothes turned dazzling white, and then Moses and Elijah showed up and started speaking with him. What a glorious vision!

You would think this would have intimidated the disciples. Yet they seemed quite comfortable. Peter even tried to start a building plan so they could preserve this experience. As rare as it is to behold a moment of glory, or a healing, or a dramatic answer to prayer, it doesn't really scare us. Frankly, we've been waiting a long time for God to do something glorious with our lives.

While Peter was making his plans, however, a cloud overshadowed the disciples. Then they became terrified. We are always more afraid of entering God's mysterious cloud than we are of beholding his glory. We enter the cloud when we are unsure of God's will or when the answer to a perfectly good request is "No."

Glorious moments are opportunities to see that God is faithful. Cloudy moments are opportunities to be faithful ourselves.

Suddenly a voice came out of the cloud and said, "This is my Son ... listen to him." Then they saw only Jesus. Whenever life gets really cloudy, and you are not sure what God is doing, just look and listen for Jesus. He can be found in the midst of every mystery. He is the only plan you need to behold God's glory.

❦

The Savior You Think You Know

"Prophets are not without honor, except in their home-town."

Mark 6:4

Read Mark 6:1-6

Jesus spoke those words after a very frustrating experience trying to minister to the people of Nazareth. By this time Jesus had taught all over Galilee. He had calmed storms, healed the sick, cast out demons, and even raised Jairus' daughter from what looked like death. Surely word about all this had reached his hometown. Yet when he went to the people who watched him grow up, we are told, "he was amazed at their unbelief." They were so focused on the carpenter that they could not see the Savior. Ironically, the people who assumed that they knew him best did not really know him even as well as the thief on the cross.

The fascinating thing about this narrative is that because the people believed they knew Jesus so well, they limited what he could do for them. No matter how much you have heard about what Jesus has done for others, the real issue is, do you believe this man you think you've known your whole life can really save you? One of the greatest dangers to being Christian is assuming too much familiarity with Jesus. If you limit him by your experiences, your theology, and your hopes and expectations, you will end up with something less than a Savior and more like a carpenter. His salvation of your life begins with the belief that there is more to Jesus than you know. If you bring the humility, he can bring the salvation.

❦

Distracted by Vision

"What is it you want me to do for you?"

Mark 10:36

READ MARK 10:35-45

As Jesus led the disciples toward Jerusalem, the seat of power, he noticed James and John were suddenly quite close to him. So he asked them, "What do you want me to do for you?" They responded by asking Jesus if they could sit on his left and right hands, once they all got to Jerusalem. It was like asking to be Jesus' chief of staff. Yet of course Jesus wasn't going to Jerusalem to run for office. He was going to die.

By the time they had traveled as far as Jericho, a great multitude of people had begun to follow this new candidate, hoping he would take power. Suddenly, a blind beggar, named Bartimaeus, cried out, "Jesus, son of David, have mercy on me." So Jesus stopped the parade and asked Bartimaeus the same question he had just asked his disciples. "What do you want me to do for you?" I've always wondered if Jesus was looking at James and John when he asked this.

How would you answer that question? Would you also ask for power? Or maybe money? Or friends? Yet Jesus is not a genie, granting three wishes. He is the Savior, dying to love you. In order to receive that salvation, you can't be distracted by your own visions of glory.

According to Mark, this is the first time Jesus is referred to as the son of David, the Savior. Isn't it interesting that it took a blind beggar to see that?

❦

How to Reach for a Savior

"Who touched me?"

Mark 5:31, RSV

READ MARK 5:25-34

A great crowd followed Jesus as he headed for the home of Jairus, a ruler of the synagogue who had a very sick daughter. Yet suddenly the excitement was interrupted by a woman who had been suffering from hemorrhages for twelve years. When she reached out to touch the hem of Jesus' garment, he stopped everything and asked, "Who touched me?"

At first this story about the woman seems out of place. The urgent matter of healing Jairus' little girl has to be put aside in order for us to consider this ordinary woman with a chronic illness. Yet the Gospel writer Mark is more interested in the crowd than he is in the big event at Jairus' home. He puts a magnifying glass up to that crowd to focus our attention on just one woman who would be so easy to overlook.

Mark does this because he believes we are all hemorrhaging. Maybe you also have a physical problem that will not go away. Or maybe you're bleeding internally from a broken heart or a broken dream. The hurt happened years ago. You've tried everything, but nothing can make the pain go away. So you join the crowds at the church, hoping to get a glimpse of this Savior. You're sure he has more important business to deal with than you. Yet if you just humbly reach out to Jesus, he will stop the whole parade. He'll eventually make it to the home of the rulers, but today Jesus is looking for you. That's because your broken life has touched him.